Flat Out

Flat Out
The Race for the Motorcycle Land Speed Record

Rocky Robinson

MOTORBOOKS

First published in 2007 by Motorbooks, an imprint of MBI Publishing Company, Galtier Plaza, Suite 200, 380 Jackson Street, St. Paul, MN 55101 USA

Motorbooks titles are also available at discounts in bulk quantity for industrial or sales-promotional use. For details write to Special Sales Manager at MBI Publishing Company, Galtier Plaza, Suite 200, 380 Jackson Street, St. Paul, MN 55101 USA.

To find out more about our books, join us online at www.motorbooks.com.

Editor: Peter Schletty
Designer: Tom Heffron

Library of Congress Cataloging-in-Publication Data

Robinson, Rocky, 1961-
  Flat out : the race for the motorcycle world land speed record / by Rocky Robinson.
    p. cm.
  ISBN-13: 978-0-7603-3163-7 (hc)
  ISBN-10: 0-7603-3163-4 (hc)
  1. Motorcycle racing. 2. Motorcycle racing--Records. 3. Robinson, Rocky, 1961- I. Title.
GV1060.R59 2007
796.75--dc22
                                        2007010123

Printed in United States of America

Contents

Acknowledgments
A Word of Thanks

This book would not be possible without the help of a lot of wonderful people I am lucky to be associated with. Had it not been for Mike Akatiff and Denis Manning giving me the opportunity to pilot their equipment, there would be no story. Thanks for giving me a chance, and thanks for all the great times we shared on and off the track.

To John Jans; not only was he instrumental in building many of the BUB streamliners, including their current ride, he also made time to help me with the writing process and accuracy of our story—and, he just happens to be a great guy. Thank you for all your help.

To the entire *Top-1 Ack Attack* Racing crew, especially Mike and Christy Akatiff, Ken Puccio, Frank Milburn, Jim and Mary True, Buzzy Mulbach, Chuck Bullwinkle, Gary Vanderpool, Jim Leal, and Greg Akatiff. You guys did all the hard work. I was the lucky one fortunate enough to be allowed behind the controls for the ultimate ride.

On the BUB team, John Jans, Howard Carte, Jeff Boyle, Joe Harrelson, and the rest. Thanks for all your hard work and for never losing sight of the dream. When things got heavy I could always count on you guys to bring a smile to my face. Though I wouldn't say you made my job easy, you kept it fun and always interesting. I respect all of you for your many talents and dedication to the team.

If it weren't for my dad, I doubt I'd have the courage to take on such a dangerous challenge. He taught me to never let fear run my life, and my only hope is that I've lived up to his expectations. He was never one to hold things back, and he always spoke his mind. At times he seemed overly critical, but that was only because he cared so much for my safety. I've never met a more talented, hard working individual in all my life. Thanks for giving so much without expecting anything in return. Because of you, I've lived a life with more opportunities than most, and lived to tell about them. It's been quite a ride and I love you for being who you are. Thanks for being a part of it every step of the way.

My mom is the flipside of my dad, and she always keeps me in check with my feelings and makes sure I have a positive attitude. She never misses a race, and is a big part of our team both emotionally and spiritually. Not to mention she is arguably the best cook on the planet. It's partially because of her that I train so hard. Mom, I love you for always taking the time to show me how much you care.

My brother Buddy is much like my dad—fearless and hard working. He is good at everything he does, and it's good to have someone like him on your side. "Whatever's too tough for them is just right for me" is his mantra. His competitive nature taught me to always push harder and never give up. Growing up with him was a blast. Thanks, bro, for looking after your little brother and making growing up so much fun.

Behind every man is a woman, and mine is truly the best. I put Tricia through hell with my racing program, but she takes it all in stride. She is my best friend and the love of my life, and is also competitive by nature. And, she loves going fast! Who could ask for more? I love you, Tricia.

There are many more who've helped me through the years: Kenny Weddingfeld, who traveled the country with me during my early flat track racing days. Scott Jensen, my best friend and someone who is always there for me. Don Eslinger, a former coworker who turned out to be so much more. Thanks to my daughter Kristin, who puts things in perspective for me, and reminds me why it is so important to always come home safely. And to Mario, my new stepson, whom I love and respect, I only hope that he will someday have some of the same opportunities I do and not take them for granted.

I will also always be grateful to our sponsors for giving us a chance to strut our stuff at their expense. Top-1 Oil paved the way for the *Ack Attack* team to find our place in history. Suzuki also played a major role, supplying motors and an abundant supply of parts. On the BUB side, Fred Fox of Lemans Corporation has been behind us from the beginning. Saddleman and Barnett, Motion Pro, Drag Specialties, Parts Unlimited, K&N and many others. You guys are the best, and we couldn't have done it without you. Thank you for your support throughout the years and for being a part of our team.

I lost my sister (Leilani Robinson) to cancer several years back and to this day have trouble accepting it. She brought two lovely daughters into the world (Cassie and Nikki) but never got the chance to watch them blossom into beautiful young women. This book is dedicated to her memory.

Introduction

S*ummer of 1999*: After a last-minute briefing, Denis wishes me luck and jumps in the duallie and heads to the far end of the course. He'll be in constant contact with the rest of the crew, but likes to position himself to watch the run uninterrupted. He's also navigating our huge enclosed race trailer, so he needs a head start to get to the other end.

For me, any hopes of traveling in comfort were immediately dismissed as John tugged and pulled at my safety harness until he was satisfied there was no means of escape. Not unlike the great Houdini, my arms and legs were restrained, my body cloaked in a thick fire-retardant suit, and a tight Nomex liner mashed against my face, making it difficult to breathe through my full-faced helmet.

As if that weren't enough, he then wedged a neck brace between my shoulders and the base of the helmet. It reminded me of the time I spent the night in the hospital strapped to a board, my neck in traction, while I waited for the specialist to arrive the next morning. Comfort in streamlined motorcycles is more of an afterthought than a necessity.

As John finished the 10-minute routine of strapping me in, I noticed the beads of sweat building around his brow. I immediately reached forward and flicked on the electric pump that filled my cool suit with ice water. Before this simple luxury, the trip was barely tolerable, due to the intense heat contained within the cockpit. But now, under a controlled environment, things were, well, cool . . .

I pulled my arms to my chest as the canopy was latched into place, completely enclosing me inside. Claustrophobia is not an option in this job description. I flip the MoTeC computer screen into warmup mode and wait for the starter to engage. After a few heavy clunks and chugs, the motor turns over freely. I flip on the ignition switch and the dead rotating mass suddenly comes to life.

The sound is amazing. Deep, loud–almost angry. At only 6 inches behind my head, I know it very well. A few seconds later the switch is flicked again, this time into race mode. It's almost show time. I can't see behind me, and peripheral vision is also somewhat limited. For that matter, looking straight ahead has its difficulties, as the long nose of the bike forces you to look far ahead, the horizon barely visible over the dash and bodywork.

John steps into my line of sight and holds up the two pins that were just pulled from the retractable skids which hold me upright until my forward momentum takes over. Without the pins removed it would be impossible for me to retract the skids into the bodywork once under way—*a definite safety factor*. He then pulls on the tether attached to the tow vehicle and instructs the driver to inch ahead until all the slack is taken up. We make eye contact as he gives me the thumbs up signal. I return the gesture as I prepare myself for something neither Disneyland nor Universal Studios has yet to re-create. This is one "E"-ticket ride, and I'm in the best seat in the house!

As the tether tightens, I take a deep breath and ready myself for a thrill only a few people have been lucky enough to experience.

The heavy mass of metal, fiberglass, and highly combustible fuel jerks forward. I favor the right skid and try to keep the machine leaned in that direction until enough momentum carries me past the need for mechanical assistance. Once that point is reached, I retract the skids and balance the machine delicately as the tow vehicle increases our speed.

A strange metamorphosis has just taken place. The second the skids left the salt, I was no longer piloting this marvel of engineering, this computerized, technologically advanced mechanical wizardry—I was riding a motorcycle. I was finally back in familiar territory, and I was liking it!

Thanks to many years chasing behind a ski boat on water skis, I was actually quite comfortable being towed by a tether attached to a rapidly accelerating motorized vehicle. Comfortable to a point that when it was time to release, I could cut across an imaginary wake of salt and slingshot myself by the tow vehicle while releasing the tether, still freewheeling out of gear.

It's time to get serious now . . . I rev the engine for good measure, and as the rpm starts to fall I engage the transmission, which simultaneously retards the ignition. This in turn offers free play in the gearbox to allow for a clean shift. The amount of torque produced by this machine in first gear is incredible. So much so that without adequate throttle control, the rear tire could light up uncontrollably. Blistered or shredded tires have no place on a machine designed to go half the speed of sound. On this machine, first gear will take you to about 160–170 mph. Not bad for a "granny gear"!

For those of you who have seen the motorcycling documentary *On Any Sunday*, the narrator described steering a streamliner, where at low speed you turned left to go right and right to go left. Once above a certain mph, he stated, the opposite was true. In my experience driving motorcycle streamliners, he wasn't telling the whole story.

What I mean to say is that, at least in my situation, I was strapped in so tight there was absolutely no room for "body English" to initiate a turn. Instead, to go right you had to first steer left, which would initiate a lean to the right. You would then follow it. The same is true to go left. Denis Manning liked to describe it as taking your hand and balancing a broomstick in your palm. To make it go left you must first move your hand to the right to initiate the lean angle. (This practice is actually true for all motorcycles, but must be more aggressively initiated in streamliners due to the lack of body English.)

The basics of steering actually *do* change at high speed, but not exactly how it was described in the movie. At high speed, there are air effect and wind drag to deal with. And this motorcycle is 20 feet long, so it is also a high-speed rolling billboard. Side winds have much more effect than on a conventional motorcycle. Anyways, back to the run . . .

We have a state-of-the-art computerized digital readout display covering everything from mph and rpm to what gear I'm in, where I'm at on the track, top attained speed, and I'm sure if there was room for it, it could even make coffee—this thing is tricked out! Indy cars and Formula One cars use a similar device.

I'm doing 160 and we're still in first gear. Shifting to second has its moments. If I shift too soon the engine could bog, too late and it over-revs. If I nail it, it's like finding that elusive sweet spot. Things get real happy!

The tranny gods are with us today, as the bike shifts flawlessly into the next cog. Life is good . . .

In second gear, the bike takes on a whole new personality. Because we now have a fair amount of momentum on our side, I can start to accelerate much more aggressively. The engine really stands on its toes and roars. The sound is much louder now. It's gone beyond the angry stage—this thing is pissed!

Hurling down the salt, I do my best to keep one eye at least occasionally focused on the speedo and wonder if it's working properly. 175, 180, 190, 200 mph and climbing like nobody's business. The rear of the bike is now in a constant drift from wheel spin, but remains stable and controllable. I plant my feet against the floorboards and push myself as high as I can to see out over the nose. I use the horizon as a point of reference. It tells me if I'm perpendicular to the ground or if I'm running dangerously askew.

As I lift myself higher in the cockpit for a better view, things suddenly become a blur. The hard shell of my helmet makes contact with the steel cage surrounding my head. The vibrations are at such a high frequency that the muscles in my eyes used for focusing cannot react fast enough. I pull my head away ever so slightly and try to regain my composure as well as my focus: 225, 235, 240—is that thing for real?!!!

Shifting gears is normally no big deal. You want to go faster, you grab a higher gear. At 240 miles an hour on a slick racing surface—while lying on your back trying to counter the constant wind shifts, it can get . . . interesting. Time is something you don't have a lot of. Ten miles of salt goes by pretty fast when you're in a hurry. I watch my horizon until I'm sure I'm perpendicular with God and the ground. I'm still holding my own between the markers on either side of the course. The tach says shift, the horizon agrees, and I'm still somewhat centered on the course . . .

"Click"

Technology is so cool. I hold the throttle pinned, push the button, and hope for the best. The shift is made cleanly, third gear and *still* picking up speed. 250, 255, 260. Either the speedo has gone bananas, or we're starting to get with the program now.

Speed does weird things to your mind. For example, the mile markers that line the course *which normally take about a minute each to pass by*, are now lining up like a picket fence. Even though the course is usually 80 to 100 feet wide (and the mile markers border each side of the course), at extreme speeds they narrow quite quickly. It feels like trying to wedge an 18-wheeler into a "compact" parking spot *with the accelerator mashed* during rush hour. Things are getting pretty busy at this point.

And then there's the wind.

One of the biggest factors in speed racing on two wheels is making a clean pass with either the wind at your back, or a direct headwind. Crosswinds are no fun and increase the pucker factor tenfold at high speed. Luckily, on this particular run the air is calm and no side winds come into play. But at 265 mph, the rate of acceleration is starting to taper. Our sleek aerodynamic shape feels like it has somehow transformed itself into that of a Mack truck bucking a serious head wind while climbing the Grapevine on I-5.

The electronic tach strains to reach redline, the speedo hovers at 270, and now both wheels are in a drift, fighting to stay in line while the mile markers start to blur along with everything else. I'm nearing the 4-mile marker and need to get in high gear soon so I can sprint through the measured mile (from the 5 to the 6) flat out.

The down-force against the nose of the bike is so great that the bike tries to wander from side to side. The slightest direction change can use up the entire width of the course before you realize it is happening. At this point I'm committed. Letting off on the throttle will only make things worse. A bike 20 feet long barreling down the salt with less than optimal traction does not like sudden changes. Just letting off on the throttle could provoke a severe weight transfer, which could overload the front end, resulting in possible tire failure or an uncontrollable speed wobble.

Instead, I stiffen my grip on the bars and press forward—the throttle still pinned. I counter every weave and actually find a rhythm that makes the ride almost predictable. The extra maneuvering and the higher wind resistance add to the bike's vibrations, taking a toll on my already limited vision.

But I'm in the zone. I can do this.

I can see the 4-mile marker coming up and verify it on the MoTeC screen. I time my rhythm with the bike's constant weave, placing us as close to the center of the course as possible, while aligning the horizon with the base of the windshield. The target centers in my cross hairs, and I fire.

One of the only real "trouble areas" we have is the transmission. On about 80 percent of our runs we've experienced a transmission failure of one sort or another. Making it through all four gears smoothly is an accomplishment for our team. Four hundred and twenty horsepower spinning a tranny faster than any other motorcycle tranny has ever spun has its difficulties. John Jans designed and built a work of art that will one day carry us to the all-time world's fastest speed record for motorcycles. But until we get there, a few improvements still need to be made and a few bugs worked out.

At this point of the game everyone involved is standing on the sidelines holding their breath. This reminds me of that old saying about knowing the difference between being involved or committed. It's like a bacon and egg breakfast. The chicken was involved, but the pig—he was committed . . . right now I'm feeling a bit committed myself. Keep in mind, most airplanes need less than half this speed to get off the ground.

I squeeze the button one final time while doing my best to keep the bike pointed somewhat centered down the course. If she shifts, we just might be making history. If she doesn't, we're toast. At least we had a complete breakfast . . .

I glance at the tach as the shift is made and the rpm drop from 8,000 to around 6,500. The speedo also drops from about 270 to 265. That brief instant the ignition retards and the tallest cog is engaged, takes its toll on our forward momentum. The wind resistance against the front of the machine is so great that it actually slows the bike down during a shift that took less than a second to transpire. The good news is the shift from third to fourth was executed perfectly. Score one "attaboy" for John!

In only a matter of seconds the 5-mile marker comes into sight. At these speeds it takes a little longer for the revs to climb, but I'm at around 7,200 rpm going into the 5-mile and approaching *280 mph*! It seems impossible, but in only seconds the 6-mile marker is already fast approaching. I take one final glance at the MoTeC as I maneuver my right hand in position to hit the high-speed parachute. In the time it takes for my eyes to leave the salt and focus on the MoTeC, and then back to the salt, nearly a half-mile has passed. To give you a model for comparison, at 300 mph you would be traveling approximately the distance of one and a half football fields per second!

My last glimpse registers 7,500 rpm and a speed of 289 mph. While the speed and rpm are still climbing, I have other concerns to deal with which are more important. A loud thump smashes against the inside of the composite body, telling me something has let go. The transmission also makes a peculiar sound that causes reason for concern. The good news is the run is just about over and for the most part, it has been a success.

With the throttle still pinned to avoid any rapid weight transfer, I deploy the high-speed chute. The 6-mile marker disappears behind me as a firm, yet steady tug pulls at the rear of the machine. At nearly 300 mph on a 2,000-pound machine, conventional brakes are pretty much useless. The tiny, 18-inch, high-speed chute creates enough drag for me to roll out of the throttle.

What happens next I can never find the right words to describe. The maximum speed indicator locked in at just over 291 mph. Not a bad run, but still a little short of the record. As I scrub off speed,

I watch the speedo while preparing to deploy the big chute. At 6 feet in diameter, this thing can be a little nasty at times. If a cross-wind comes up, it will pull the rear of the bike in whatever direction it is blowing. If I pull the chute too soon, at too high a rate of speed, it can literally rip the bike in two. If the parachute fails, I have one spare, provided they don't become tangled.

A lot of information dances around in the back of your mind about all the possibilities. But at the same time, you want to get this thing stopped—preferably with the shiny side up. I wait until we're slowed up to a cool 270 mph. I brace myself and once again check to make sure I'm as perpendicular to the salt as possible. I maneuver as close to center as I can, take a deep breath, and throw out the anchor . . .

If you've ever wondered what it's like to deploy a parachute while riding a motorcycle at a high rate of speed, trust me, you better be strapped in! After the pilot chute rips the big guy from its cartridge, there's about a two-second delay before it opens and pulls tight against the tether. At about 265 mph, my harness suddenly tightens into a death-grip around my shoulders and torso. At precisely the same time, my body tries in vain to fly forward out the Plexiglas windshield directly in front of my face. My eyes bulge in my head as it's thrown forward and down against my chest.

For a brief moment, I'm not even watching where I'm going. It really wouldn't matter anyway, as there isn't much I can do until the initial "hit" is over. If you did it right up to this point, things tend to sort themselves out anyway. The rate of deceleration is incredible. I can actually slow the thing down from 265 to about 165 in a little over a half a mile. *I cover more ground than that from the time I deploy the shoot until it opens some three seconds later.* The feeling is incredible, sort of like running head-on into an airbag a half-mile deep!

The job now is to just stay in front of the parachutes. If it pulls right, I crab over to the right. Same if it pulled left. With the parachutes out, it always feels like the rear end is high and the front buried into the ground. The sensation eases as the speed drops away. At around 80–90 mph, I can finally ease into the rear brakes. They aren't overly powerful, but they get the job done eventually.

I try several times to disengage the transmission, but for whatever reason the thing won't budge. I manually engage the clutch to hopefully minimize the damage already done. Below about 50 mph, the heat and smoke from the engine compartment creeps into the cockpit with me. I'm always concerned if there's a fire, or leaking oil or fuel which could ignite, but that's just an overactive imagination on my part. The crew did a hell of a job, and this run was pretty damn fast—record or not.

Around 20 miles an hour the thing gets a little squirrelly, so I deploy the skids. This little safety net really isn't needed until the very end—as I can usually bring her to a complete stop on my own before gently easing her over onto it. It always feels like the thing will tip right over, but it doesn't . . . *most of the time.*

I cut the engine just before she stops and I'm thankful for a little bit of quiet time. No sooner had the wheels quit turning, the smell of hot oil and methanol crept silently inside with me. A haze of smoke followed, which signaled me it was time to get out. I unstrap my harness and release the hatch for some fresh air. The crew arrives and helps me out. Denis immediately takes me aside for a debriefing of the run while it's all still fresh in my memory. In the meantime the crew loads the bike in the trailer for the 5-mile haul back to the pits. All in all, not a bad day at the office.

Part One

Tenacious II: The Early Years

Chapter One
The Offer

We've all had periods in our life we wish we could do over again, or at least leave out. I was going through one of those periods when I went to work at BUB Enterprises, where I met Denis Manning. My marriage was on the rocks, my sister was dying from breast cancer, and I still wasn't over the fact that my mom and dad had finally called it quits. That, and the fact that I left our family-owned business in Salinas, California, before my brother and I killed each other. We took over the business when my dad retired and bumped heads every step of the way. I loved

The salt, perfectly flat and crunchy and worn down by the winds. Perfect.
Photo courtesy of Jean Turner

my brother, but knew if I stayed we would end up hating each other. Talk about sibling rivalry . . .

It was an all-time low in my life and my career. Denis hired me on as a welder and promised me he could keep me working for at least three months. During that time we got to know each other better and found that we both had a love for racing motorcycles. My racing background included flat racing in the Camel Pro Series on mile and half-mile dirt track ovals. I also raced Speedway for several years and won the championship in northern California in 1989. I also dabbled in trials competition competing locally, and even placed in the top three in my class at the Schreiber Cup Nationals before hanging up my boots.

Denis was more at home on the drag strip and at the local road race course. He also tried his hand at dirt track racing, but his large stature put him at a disadvantage that he wasn't able to overcome. He decided to put his talents to better use as a builder and tuner, and leave the riding to those better suited for the task.

One day his father took him to the famed Bonneville Salt Flats in Utah where he witnessed Mickey Thompson blazing down the salt at a record pace. He was immediately hooked and found a new goal in life. He would attempt to build the world's fastest motorcycle and try to capture the world land speed record for two wheels. After a few failed attempts, in 1970 he achieved his goal with the help of the Harley Davidson factory, and one of their own riders—the late Cal Rayborn. They went just over 265 mph.

As the saying goes, records were made to be broken, and it was only a matter of time before there was somebody faster. It's been more than 30 years now, and Denis is still trying to recapture the record. He's closer now than ever before . . .

So I put in my three months welding exhaust pipes and learning the trade. It didn't take long before I was managing the shop and running a small crew. That was almost 15 years ago—I guess I passed the audition . . .

We'd all be going wide open in the shop, banging out parts like crazy. Denis would be locked away in his office making drawing after drawing of his new streamliner. The shop wasn't very big, but still had to do double-duty as a manufacturing facility and a race shop. I was always being called upon to weld this, or fabricate that, anything he needed to keep moving forward with his racing effort. I thought it was all pretty cool, but still wasn't really into his world of land speed racing.

Then one day that all changed.

I remember being in the dumps about my soon-to-be ex filing for divorce. A friend of mine, Steve Erwin, was going through the same thing, so we planned on moving in together until we both got back on our feet. It seemed we had a lot in common. We were both in the motorcycle industry. He worked for Tucker-Rocky as a sales rep. We also both rode trials at the time. Still another thing we shared was that we were both married to good housekeepers. As it turned out, both our ex-wives got to keep our houses! Such is life . . .

I had just finished welding my zillionth header together when Denis called me into his office. He had this big grin on his face that had me wondering what was going on. These weren't exactly happy times for me. "Sit down," he ordered politely. I tried to read his thoughts but was coming up empty.

I remember him saying something to the effect of, "You know, I had originally planned on racing the new streamliner myself . . . but my family doesn't think that's such a good idea. The business is growing and I'm not getting any younger." Right then I knew what was coming next. "What would you think of driving it for me?"

Up until recently, I didn't even know what a streamliner was. My kind of racing always involved banging handlebars and eating dirt. This was uncharted territory for me. I wasn't sure if getting the opportunity to rub salt in my wounds was entirely in my best interest. I decided I'd need some time to think it over. I sat back in my chair and took a deep breath. "Yeah, I'll do it."

So much for thinking it over. The timing was just right. I wasn't thrilled with my life in its current state. My attitude was sort of haphazard. I didn't really care that I would be putting my life on the line. I had a beautiful daughter and wonderful stepson that I loved and cared about, but I didn't care about myself. I needed this as much as Denis needed me. The deal was done.

From that moment on I became much more involved in the racing part of BUB Enterprises. Denis and I discussed everything from aerodynamics to parachutes. It was his job to get the thing built, but mine to be prepared when the time came to put it to the test.

One of the things that helped a great deal was my involvement in trials competition. Oddly enough, riding a motorcycle capable of speeds of less than zero (I could make the thing go backward if I wanted to) had its advantages. A sense of balance is everything, and nowhere else can you better hone your skills for balancing a motorcycle than in trials. You learn to do things on a bike that you would swear were impossible. And once you become comfortable doing so, you tend to push the limits even farther.

I remember on one occasion at Bonneville we were having trouble keeping enough compressed air onboard to deploy the skids at the end of a run to keep the bike upright until it comes to a stop. As I coasted down to about 20 mph, I flipped the switch that deploys the skids. There wasn't enough air left in the system for deployment. I flipped the switch back and forth hoping I'd get lucky. As the miles per hour continued to fall, I countered every lean until I'd brought the bike to a complete stop—upright and with no skids!

A second later it dropped on its side, like a drunken biker coming to a stop and forgetting to put his foot down. It was an embarrassing moment for both the crew and myself, but at least I was able to keep damage to a minimum and walk away unharmed.

I also did a lot of road riding on the shop's Harley Dresser to get comfortable with manhandling a heavy machine. We live up in the foothills of Grass Valley, where there are a lot of tight, twisty sections of road where I could put the heavy cruiser through its paces at speeds well above its intended use. Probably not the most responsible thing to do, but at least I was out in the boonies by myself where I wasn't a danger to anybody else.

There's no real training program for racing streamliners because so few actually do it. I've always been a fanatic about staying fit, but getting used to going 300-plus, only inches off the ground, while lying on your back—how do you train for that?! In the motorcycle streamliner racer's handbook most of the pages are blank. We intend to fill them in as we go. I hope this book answers a lot of the questions along the way . . .

Chapter Two
Tenacious II Gets Put Through the Paces

The streamliner was named *Tenacious II*, which followed in the footsteps of a previous effort that ended with a crashed motorcycle. Denis decided to retain the same basic shape, color scheme, and name, but everything else was either redesigned or improved upon.

One of the big changes was to veer away from center-hub steering. It was commonly used in streamlined motorcycles because it took up less space than conventional, telescopic forks. The tradeoff, according to Denis, was marginal steering

The view from downtown Wendover as we headed out to the salt each morning to chase our dreams. *Photo courtesy of Tricia Robinson*

capabilities and the lack of "feel" one is accustomed to with a more traditional front end. A "leading link" design was used instead. It had many advantages over center-hub steering. It was more stable at speed and easier to control. It was also tunable, which made it more user-friendly when course conditions were less than desirable.

The powerplant for *Tenacious II* is another story all its own. A V-4 layout was used to minimize both weight and space. The engine was designed from scratch, unlike the original *Tenacious* project, which utilized a modified Harley Davidson replica engine built by S&S motors.

For all you gearheads out there, let me go into further detail about the engine. Again, keep in mind that this motor started out as a clean sheet of paper and is not a copy of any existing motorcycle engine, nor is it a modified car engine of any kind. In fact, probably the only off-the-shelf parts used were the Carrillo connecting rods.

Denis Manning and Joe Harrelson collaborated on the basics, but it was Joe's engineering background that made it happen. A college professor at UC Davis, Joe is one of those brainiac types with moments of pure genius. Creating *Medusa,* the name fondly given to *Tenacious II*'s powerplant, was one of those moments.

In original form the all-aluminum, 3,000-cc behemoth put out 420 horsepower at 8,000 rpm. It utilized dual-overhead cams, was naturally aspirated, and water-cooled. A MoTeC electronic fuel injection system insured proper air/fuel mapping of the methanol fuel. The torque of this motor in original form was a staggering 299 lb-ft with a brake mean effective pressure (BMEP) of 242. This translates to 2.34 horsepower per cubic inch. For comparison, the Harley Davidson Evolution motor, at 80 cubic inches, puts out approximately 0.65 horsepower per cubic inch.

Medusa is one highly efficient piece of machinery! As you'll read later on, these numbers were improved upon substantially.

I remember the day I first met Joe. Denis was describing him to me before he arrived. He said he even looked the part of your typical college professor (if there was that sort of thing). He wore thick glasses, had messy hair, and matching pocket protectors on each side of his shirt filled with pens and various measuring devices. Denis described this to me as "total frontal nerdity." While that may have been the case, he is a very likable guy and a key ingredient to our racing team. Without him I don't know if we could have accomplished our goals in the manner in which we did.

There's a lot of cool onboard gadgetry, and the MoTeC digital readout display has got to top the list—at least from a driver's point of view. It is what connects me to the bike, the track, and the run itself. A black wand displays the rpm as it climbs steadily between shifts. Wheel spin or a slipping clutch can also be acknowledged through this same display. The speedometer pulls double duty, showing active speed and top speed. The gear selection is also displayed, as well as an odometer that is reset before each run.

The odometer is a very crucial instrument in land speed racing. At high speeds, due to high frequency vibrations, it is difficult to focus outside the vehicle. The mile markers can sometimes become difficult, if not impossible to read. The odometer tells you precisely where you are at all times. In Australia, they had the course laid out entirely different to what we are used to here at home. It was confusing and poorly done compared to the standards we've become accustomed to stateside. The odometer allowed me to bypass their entire marking system and still know precisely where I was, restoring my confidence, which otherwise would have surely waned.

You may have seen our digital display, or one similar to it, if you've ever watched Formula 1 racing on television. The display screen attached to their steering wheel is virtually the same as what we are using. The feedback from the tiny screen is invaluable in high-speed racing.

The braking system is another oddity of our machine. On a more conventional motorcycle, hydraulic disc brakes are the norm, but even the older drum design still works well on less sophisticated machines. I can honestly say, on my very first test run, I questioned the performance of our braking system. The rear wheel has state-of-the-art hydraulic discs—but in my opinion, they just plain sucked.

I was towed to about 65 miles per hour before releasing from the tow vehicle. When I did, I freewheeled for several miles before hitting the brakes and bringing her to a stop. This test was done dead-engine. We were evaluating the balance of the bike, the steering, and the braking—and also the lack of vision from the cockpit. Everything we did, we did in stages. Our testing procedures, though somewhat limited, were very thorough.

So after the bike finally slowed to about 30 miles per hour, I squeezed the hand-operated brake lever to bring the beast to a stop. The brakes dragged and did slow the bike down, eventually getting the job done. *Eventually* is the key word here. I mean, I was only doing 30, but it seemed like a major strain to bring its aluminum billet wheels to rest.

I remember immediately complaining to Denis about their poor performance. Oddly enough, he was actually amused with my apparent disappointment. His response reminded me of one of my favorite scenes from the movie *Blazing Saddles*, when several groups of bad guys were being deputized so they could take over the town and its sheriff. A small group of banditos had just been sworn in and handed their badges. They tossed them in the dirt in defiance. It was a parody of a similar scene in the classic film *The Treasure of the Sierra Madre*. "Badges. We don't need no stinking badges!" They fired their guns into the air and laughed at the *federales*.

My evaluation of his response had a very similar tone. "Brakes. We don't need no stinking brakes! Wait until you try the parachutes."

That's right. Parachutes. How many motorcycles have you seen with parachutes as their chief source of braking? I couldn't quite get it through my head that driving a motorcycle at around 300 miles per hour doesn't require any brakes!

"Simply deploy the parachutes and you'll be fine."

Sure. No problem . . .

And then there's the skids.

I've ridden all kinds of motorcycles in my career. Flat trackers, short trackers, TT bikes, speedway bikes, and even trials bikes. And tons of streetbikes, and dirt bikes too. Not one of them had retractable skids to keep the bike upright at low speeds.

That is, until I started racing streamliners. When you're strapped inside, there's no way to put your foot down. That can pose a problem if the goal is to keep the shiny side up. *Tenacious II* was 20 feet long. It had a steel chassis enclosed in a fiberglass body. I was strapped in so tight with leg restraints, arm restraints, etc., that even if there was a place to stick my foot out, I probably couldn't hold her up. Plus, the thing weighed nearly 2,000 pounds with me in it. I don't think my Alpine Star racing sneakers were designed to carry that much load!

The skids were a must. They were designed like miniature out-riggers with steel skids welded on the bottom to glide along the salt at reasonably slow speeds. Basically the same idea as training wheels on your first bicycle—except a metal ski replaced the wheel, and they were retractable. Show up with a pair of these on your Stingray at your buddy's fifth-year birthday party and you were guaranteed all the gumballs and Dr. Pepper you could stomach!

When I was being towed at the beginning of a run, I could usually retract them at about 20–25 mph. They had pneumatic rams attached to them that brought them inside the fiberglass body. Large sheetmetal flaps then closed over them, keeping the shape more aerodynamic. At the end of the run I'd deploy them once again. Ease her gently over and bring her to rest. Sounds so simple, doesn't it?

Not exactly.

The skids do work fine, and we're always trying to improve upon them, but we've had our share of *moments* because of them. Here's just the short list from the top of my head:

Moment No. 1: Our First Crash!

It was our first trip to Bonneville with the new bike. The design was new, the crew was basically new, and learning all the new procedures was, well . . . *new*. When the bike was resting on the skids, we had pins that locked them into place so they couldn't retract unexpectedly. I was sitting in the cockpit, getting used to my new surroundings. The bike had just been set on the ground and we were getting ready to make our first tow test. Everyone was busy getting ready. There was a lot to do.

It would have been nice if somebody had put the pins in place to keep the bike from falling over. In slow motion, the bike started to lean over. Our boys gallantly came to my rescue and quickly decided to manhandle the 20-foot, 2,000-pound machine back upright.

Did I mention this thing was pretty aerodynamically shaped? This means everything is smooth . . . no handles or anything to grab onto! Try as they might, *Tenacious II* recorded its first crash while still in the pits at approximately 0 mph. (I wonder if that's a record . . .)

Moment No. 2: Our 2nd Crash!

A new procedure had been designed to ensure that this silly incident would never happen again. The pins had long fluorescent ribbons attached to them. Whenever the skids were deployed and the bike was stationary, the pins were *in*. Right before each run, John Jans would stand just in front of my windshield and hold the pins in front of him for me to see. This signaled that all systems were *go* and the pins were pulled. It was time to go racing.

Did I mention the skids used an overcenter cam design? This meant that once the skids were deployed, everything was fine . . . unless you rolled backward. Thrilled with having made one of my first runs over 200 mph, I proudly threw out the laundry (parachutes) and brought *Tenacious II* promptly to a stop with finesse and grace. She leaned over effortlessly onto the right side skid and stopped precisely as planned. I was jazzed. I reached for my harness release to escape from my restraints. That's when I heard it . . .

I usually hold on the brakes until someone comes to my aid to help me out of my tight confines. In earlier testing, we had an aborted run that barely went over 160 mph. I didn't think it was even fast enough to necessitate using the chutes—so I didn't. Did I mention my previous feelings about this machine's brakes? With no parachutes, and only the rear disc brake to bring me to a stop, it took much longer than I expected. When it finally did, I held the brakes firm, waiting for someone to come to my rescue.

Unknown to me, a fire had started in the rear of the bike from the brakes becoming so damned hot. As I squeezed the lever against the bar, suddenly all the pressure went away. The bike rolled backward slightly, which brought the skids back overcenter and automatically retracted them. But I can't blame this one on the skids. This was due to our state-of-the-art, hydraulic disc brakes. "Brakes. We don't need no stinking brakes!" I heard it again . . .

Anyway, I'm sitting there basking in my glory of just making the 200 mph club. I was the man! As I undid my harness release so I could get out and make sure somebody noticed, I heard a faint "click," signaling I was in trouble. In all my excitement, I had forgotten to hold onto the brake (me and that damned brake) and as I reached for my harness release, the movement must have been just enough to back up the skids past center. Wham! Crash No. 2 by reason of skids (and pilot error) was recorded. Keep in mind that we have yet to crash at over 1 mph!

Moment No. 3: A Crash Avoided—By Using the Skids!!!

At our first Utah Salt Flats Racing Association (USFRA) meet, rain had made the course nearly impossible for the motorcycles. The cars did okay, but chewed up the course, leaving deep ruts and holes for us to contend with. I remember making a fairly slow pass, less than 200 mph. I was struggling to keep the bike upright. The front tire kept catching the ruts and sending me off course. I backed out of the throttle before realizing it was too late. I was going to go down, and probably pretty hard. I threw out the laundry, but now at only 160 or so they had much less effect than at full speed.

Nothing seemed to help. I was forced to steer much more erratically just to keep my balance. I tried to steer the bike as close to the center of the course as I could. I nailed a deep rut at about the same time—that nearly put me on my side. I watched my horizon until I was sure I was as perpendicular to the salt as I could get. I prepared myself for disaster and flipped the switch to deploy the skids.

I kept it balanced between them for a couple of seconds, with the skids hovering dangerously close to the salt's abrasive surface. This wouldn't last long. Finally, the left skid made solid contact. THUD! It hit so hard I was afraid it might have ripped the thing clear off. Steering left shifted the weight to the other side. The right skid sort of glanced off the ground before I managed to balance it upright once again. It slowed quickly, in an awkward, wobbly sort of way.

There was no other option than to ease it back over onto the right skid and bring it to rest. There was no way I was going to risk putting it back over on the left side. For all I knew, the entire outrigger could be gone. As luck would have it, when it rolled to a stop we were still sitting shiny side up. I squeezed the brake and leaned to the right until someone came to my aid. The left skid had actually prevented an ugly crash, but was destroyed in the process.

Moment No. 4: Still More Skid-Induced Crashes!

We've had our share of bad luck during SpeedWeek at Bonneville. We usually try to run on private time, but conflicting dates, limited racing budgets, and various other excuses found us waiting in line to test our goods alongside everybody else on more than one occasion. Conditions need to be just right to go 300-plus on two wheels, and running on a course with several hundred other entrants usually makes for less than optimum racing conditions. I feel very fortunate that we get to do most of our running alone, but there have been interesting moments following the herd across the salt . . .

On one such occasion, we didn't make it past the second mile marker before taking salt samples and destroying some of the fiberglass bodywork on the left side. No sooner had the tow strap been released and the throttle barely twisted, than the rear tire broke loose and started to fishtail to the right. I was only doing about 65 when the rear passed me by. By then it was obvious we were going down, so I did the best I could to keep from high-siding. When the slick body surface finally made contact with the famed Bonneville salt, it slid on its side gracefully for nearly a quarter-mile. Friction finally overcame inertia and brought our wounded racer to rest. This was our first (and hopefully last) crash at any kind of speed at all.

We limped her back to the pits and assessed the damages. A chunk of fiberglass was busted and torn, and had to be removed. We needed something to replace the missing body panel, but were limited on resources and time. Luckily (for us anyway), George

Field's modified coupe was charging down the course at a high rate of speed. After crossing the lights, his driver chopped the throttle and all hell broke loose. The car went into a spin. As it was coming back around it caught air—big time. It flew 10–15 feet in the air (maybe higher), and flipped upside down right in front of us!

The crash looked awful. Parts were scattered everywhere. A wheel rolled silently down the course as everything else came to a screeching halt. The crowd *oohed* and *awwed*, fearing the worst. Denis and I felt for the driver and his crew, but shared other concerns.

About 30 minutes later, the twisted heap of sheet metal and steel tubing was dragged into the pits. It was literally twisted into a pile of scrap metal. The motor had rotated within the chassis. The carburetor and exhaust pipes were ripped from their original locations. The wheels were torn off, and the entire bodywork enclosing the driver was completely gone.

Luckily, the roll cage held up fairly well. It is my belief that this was what saved the driver's life. He escaped relatively unharmed. He had lost consciousness for a brief moment, but by the time they had his car back in the pits, he was walking about, trying to figure what went wrong.

Denis and I came over to examine the wreckage. We saw the driver watching a replay of the crash through somebody's video camera. What happened next was both humorous, and necessary. We approached the driver and the owner of the car. "Looks like you're all done," Denis commented politely.

"Yeah, it looks that way." Their response carried a weary tone.

Denis then reached down into the twisted heap of what had been a beautiful racing machine, and yanked loose a piece of its aluminum bodywork. "I guess you won't be needing this, then . . . "

The driver and owner looked at us awkwardly.

"We had a crash of our own, earlier. We need to make repairs to the bodywork so we can get back out there." Denis looked them both straight in the eye. We were all racers. They knew the situation well enough. They wished us luck and left in search of shade to watch more of the videotape. It was kind of a funny situation, but I'm sure we would have done the same for them had the roles been reversed.

We thrashed for hours and finally had *Tenacious II* ready for action. What we didn't realize was that underneath the repaired bodywork, other damage had been done. On our next pass, and a few more after that, the skids performed poorly. We would lose air pressure by the end of the run, making it difficult for the skids to deploy. If they did, sometimes they would collapse before the bike came to a complete stop. The air rams were finally replaced and the linkage revamped before our confidence in our high-tech training wheels was finally restored. It's amazing how something which seemed so insignificant could play such a big role in hampering the success of our mission.

Chapter Three
Our First Time

Everybody remembers their first time. It has a sentimental value that cannot be replaced no matter how many times the act is repeated: The nervous anticipation. Sleepless nights spent dreaming about what it will be like. You know what I'm talking about. That first kiss. The first time behind the wheel of your parent's car. Your first date. The first time you have sex.

Your first trip to Bonneville to drive a 300-mile-per-hour motorcycle . . .

Well, four out of five ain't bad. I remember our first trip to the salt flats like it was yesterday. I rode with Denis (actually, the only

The world famous Bonneville Salt Flats. *Photo courtesy of Larry Bliss*

time I rode with Denis), trying to pick his brain about what I could expect. He had never driven this particular streamliner, so even he wasn't sure what would happen.

Technically he *did* drive it once. But that was before it had an engine. It really *did* have training wheels at that point. He coasted it down a country road on this huge outrigger bolted on with wheels attached on either side. I never understood why he did it. The cows seemed a little surprised as well, staring at this weird contraption with this large man inside, wobbling silently down the road. They never said anything though, so I guess it was okay.

The drive took about eight hours from Grass Valley to Bonneville, but for me the time flew by. We discussed everything. What the salt lake's surface was like. The wind. The odds of it raining while we were there. (Actually, the odds were usually pretty high.) What we expected to achieve on this first trip. What to do to avoid crashing. What not to do. What type of blood I had. What the hell I was getting into. Like I said, we discussed everything.

And then we were there.

This long, narrow frontage road just stopped at the edge of the lakebed. There was a wooden sign at the end welcoming everyone who made the journey to the famed Bonneville Salt Flats. We got out and took a quick look around.

It was amazing. Bright, white, salt for as far as the eye could see. We walked out onto it and kicked and skidded our feet across the hard, abrasive surface. "Taste it." Denis encouraged.

"What?"

"Go ahead. Taste it."

I watched as he drug his finger across the ground, put it to his lips, and smiled.

"This here's the real thing, baby."

His smile grew even wider. Some people have a love affair with chocolate. For others it might be sailing, or even old movies. This guy honestly loved Bonneville. You could see it in his eyes. You could see it in the tattered straw hat he wore *only* at Bonneville. You could hear it in his voice whenever he spoke about this far-away place. He was home.

As for me, I needed a beer . . .

* * *

They say timing is everything. When you're staying in Wendover, Nevada (especially at the Stateline Casino Hotel), your timing is all screwed up. The massive casino hotel was built on the border between Nevada and Utah. There is a one-hour time difference between where you have your morning coffee, and where you drop your first quarter—all under one roof.

The plan was to get up at the crack of dawn and meet for breakfast by six o'clock. Some of our fun-loving crew felt obligated to donate half a week's salary to the one-armed bandits while downing free stale beer until the wee hours of the night. Rumor had it there was an exotic dancing establishment just down the street. In spite of our obvious love for the arts, we came here with a job to do. There were no self-indulging prima donnas on our team. We had to remain focused. (Besides, nobody knew how to get there.)

At five o'clock, my alarm went off. Seconds later I received a wake-up call from the front desk. I was tired, but excited. This would be my first big day testing on the world famous Bonneville Salt Flats. I showered and shaved and dressed in record time. How fitting, considering where I was at . . .

The restaurant seemed nearly deserted. I checked table after table. My crew had overslept. I told myself it wasn't a big deal. At least *I* was ready. I was doing *my* part. I sat and waited for the for-eign-looking waitress to notice me. I needed coffee. Intravenous would be just fine. Hook me up, please.

It took nearly 30 minutes before I saw a face I recognized. Jeff Boyle and John Jans arrived together. They noticed my half-empty cup of reheated coffee. "You're here early." Jeff sympathized.

"Early? It's six thirty. Where is everybody?"

Jeff and John looked at me somewhat amused. "It's only five thirty. We're still on Nevada time, you know."

"More coffee, please!"

* * *

The large granules of salt crunched and crumbled under our tires as our caravan proceeded in single file across the open plain. It was like being on the moon—everything was white. We followed the levee for several miles. There were a few old drags, rotting drums, and various other retired course maintenance items lining the embankment of the levee.

We pulled up next to the "short course" which had been used for a recent meet. It had big black lines laid down marking the course. It was three lanes wide with no traffic. This was better than the freeway!

While the boys readied the trailer and put up the awning, it was my job to inspect the course. Denis and I jumped in one of the cars and sped down track. It's amazing what you can learn just by having a look. For about the first quarter-mile there were lots of ruts and black rubber from spinning tires. After that it smoothed out for a ways. Occasionally you would see a big black patch on the salt and tire tracks veering off into the rough. This was where someone had lost an engine and the oil bled out the bottom.

There were veins puckering up from the smooth salt surface in random patterns. In some spots they were an inch high. We stopped to have a closer look. They were hard and jagged, but nothing we couldn't handle. There were also a few rough sections where water backed up against the levee spilled out onto the course. This would definitely make for a rough ride, but I would later learn that when you got going really fast, you only hit the high spots. Other than a few oversized potholes that we had to fill, and removing bits of debris that the other racers had left as tokens of runs gone bad, the 7-mile course was ready for action.

The crew worked well together and had everything ready for our first test within a couple of hours. If you were going to attempt to eventually go over 300 mph on a bike you've never ridden, on a surface you've never been on, what would you test first? Well, if it were up to me, I'd test those lousy brakes!

Denis decided that was fair enough. But instead of testing the wheel brakes, he wanted me to experience the power of air brakes. I was going to get my first lesson in Parachutes 101.

Vern Brown had a Chevy Extra Cab pickup that we were using for the tow vehicle at the time. Denis instructed me to jump in the back with one of the big chutes. The idea was to tie it off to the trailer hitch. Vern would take off, and when he got up to about 50 mph, I was to throw the parachute out the back. His intention was for me to see the parachute open up firsthand. He wanted me to feel the power of the chute's pulling against the truck as the air rushed in and filled its nylon web. Then I would be confident. I would finally realize what he was trying to tell me all along. "Brakes. We don't need no stinking brakes!"

Yeah, right.

Vern jumped in the cab of his truck and fired it up. I jumped into the back of the truck with the huge parachute draped over my shoulder. The parachute harness was looped around the hitch, and the crew was standing by. They too wanted to see firsthand the power of these magnificent air brakes.

Vern rolled slowly away from our pit area. His speed increased smoothly and steadily. I braced myself as I readied the parachute for flight. When Vern reached the intended speed, he tapped the horn, signaling me it was time.

Denis was a proud man. He'd show us a thing or two about streamliners. He was the master, and I was his eager pupil. I fearlessly threw the military surplus parachute into the air. If it was good enough for our fearless fighting men, it was damn sure good enough for us. As it floated through the air, I had visions of the great "Big Daddy," Don Garlits, burning down the drag strip ungodly fast. His parachutes would burst open at the end of the run, clutching him from danger and bringing him safely back to a mortal pace.

Our parachute floated into space, but never opened. It then wadded in a lump and fell awkwardly to the ground. It landed with a soft "thud" against the salt's rock-hard surface. We didn't slow down much. In fact, I don't think we slowed down at all. It was a good show though. I knew that by the expressions on our crew's faces. They were all laughing! I think I could hear Vern laughing. Denis tried not to, but he was laughing, too. The parachute harness had slipped from the trailer hitch unnoticed.

My first experience with parachutes had me wishing we had better brakes . . .

The next step was to do a dead engine tow test. The idea was to pull me up to about 65 mph and have me release and freewheel for a few miles. I would then brake and slow to a stop. We wouldn't be going near fast enough to try the parachutes yet, but that was fine with me. From what I'd seen of them so far, I would probably have better luck dragging my feet anyway.

Connecting the tow strap to the bike was always a little tricky. Inserting the nylon strap into the cam-lock mechanism always took 5 to 10 minutes just to get it fed in properly. The mechanism we used was made from a motorcycle tie down. I could release the strap by reaching up and pushing a control lever with my left leg. For a first effort, it really was sort of tricky. Over time it would be refined and made more user-friendly.

This would be a full dress rehearsal. I put on my fireproof racing suit, which was a good one—1 inch thick and hotter than hell.

Next came my Alpine Star Nomex sneakers, ear plugs, and a Nomex liner which I wore underneath my helmet—standard issue for top fuel drag racing. I'm pretty sure my Calvin Klein skivvies weren't up to code, as I had experienced minor blow-outs in the past.

I climbed in the cramped compartment, tweaking and contorting until my upper torso was resting flat against the fiberglass molded shell, encapsulating me from the harsh outside environment. John was in charge of strapping me in and making sure everything was right and safe before each run. The procedure took a good 10 minutes to perform. There were shoulder straps to latch, a lap belt, leg restraints, arm restraints, my neck brace (gag), and release straps that all had to be placed within my limited reach.

Every minute brought on increased anxiety. I could hardly move or breathe, which I was told was for my own safety. When it was finally done, the hatch was closed and for the first time I was all alone. I turned the bars from lock to lock, making sure my arm restraints had just enough play to allow for the entire steering radius to be used if necessary. After that I sat quietly. Alone.

A few minutes later, John received notice that the course was clear and we were ready to give her a go. The heat inside had become intense. So much so that the shield on my helmet was starting to fog. I wasn't too concerned since I was sure the second we started rolling the air movement inside would clear away any built- up condensation. John bent down out of my sight, and returned to my view holding the two skid pins. He really didn't need to remove them, as I had no intention of raising the skids on my first pass.

"You ready?" he asked confidently. It was easy to hear him since, at least on this pass, there would be no engine noise. I gave him the thumbs up and prepared myself for the first real step toward one day possibly being the fastest in the world on two wheels. Way cool . . .

Vern eased slowly forward under John's command. When the slack was taken from the nylon strap, he told Vern to hold up. He gave me the thumbs up once again, and jumped in the passenger side of the truck.

The strap tightened and for the first time, I was rolling in a forward direction in a streamlined motorcycle on the Bonneville Salt Flats! It felt really awkward at first, trying to counter this 20-foot-long bike as it bobbed and weaved ever so slightly. When the right skid dragged, I steered right. When the left skid dragged, I steered left. Whichever direction I steered brought an opposite lean angle. Okay . . . this was starting to make sense.

After steering left to lean the bike right, I could follow it to the right, initiating a right turn. Same was true for the left. The more drastic a turn I needed to make, I found could be made by countersteering more aggressively. *You know what?* I thought. *I can do this. This isn't so bad . . . I could do this!*

Our acceleration steadily increased. As we picked up momentum I noticed my job becoming steadily easier. I was offering less input and was now able to keep the bike upright and the skids off the salt. It was never *neutral,* but it *was* getting easier.

Visibility was always borderline, the horizon being barely visible over the long, extended fiberglass nose. Now I have this large truck in front of me blocking any view of the course I might have otherwise enjoyed. But that part's okay. I'm used to water skiing behind a boat that does the same thing. The only real difference is now I'm getting sprayed by salt rather than water from my tow vehicle. The view's not as nice either. There's usually at least one bikini-clad occupant in the boat at all times. All I've got to look at now is the back of Vern and John's heads, and this big, black truck—and my shield is still fogged up.

I watch my speedometer as it climbs to about 40 mph. I'm very conscious that one wrong move could have the skids digging into the salt and bringing me tumbling to the ground. At 50, I release. The two heads and the big, black truck ease to the left of the course and follow at a safe distance.

Once on my own, I realize I've gained complete control. I can see the bright, white salt stretching out for miles in front of me. I can see the course markers easy enough, too. I try to relax and enjoy the ride. The second I do, I lose the horizon! Slumping even half an inch allows the horizon to disappear just below the long nose of our stretched-out machine. With no horizon, it makes it difficult to maintain balance. The left skid nicks the salt and sends me into a slight wobble.

I stomp my feet into the footrests and push my head up high, bottoming my helmet out against the top of the roll cage. The horizon returns, along with my confidence. I keep the bike centered between the skids for the rest of the run, never touching the salt again until the bike rolls to a complete stop. The test proves to us just how aerodynamic *Tenacious II* really is. Releasing at only 50 mph, we were able to coast for over 3 1/2 miles without the use of the motor. I probably could have gone a little farther, but only a little . . .

We wheeled the bike back into the pits and readied it for what we all came for. Our first *real* run under power from the mighty *Medusa*.

Every time the oversized powerplant was fired, it drew a crowd—in the parking lot of our shop, in the dyno room, and at the various motorcycle shows we were later invited to so others could see the mighty machine up close and personal.

Today would not be that day.

As we all prepared for the big moment, something went wrong that put an end to our hopes of making that first powered run. An external starter is used to turn over the massive flywheels and breathe fire into the powerful V-4 engine. John connected the coupler from the starter motor to the large hex nut at the end of the crankshaft. When he squeezed the trigger on the starter motor, rather than spin the motor to life, it spun the end of the crankshaft right off!

We were all devastated. We drove 500 miles to Bonneville to make one 50-mile-per-hour pass with a dead engine. It was a start, but we all wanted more. Denis, being the eternal optimist, decided to turn a negative into a positive. He knew there was no way to make a run under power . . . but that didn't mean we couldn't make a few more dead-engine passes and become more familiar with the new racer. We were already here, we had a job to do, and Denis helped us to realize it wasn't over.

We prepped the bike and made three or four more dead-engine runs. By the second attempt, I had pulled in the skids for the first time and balanced *Tenacious II* for the entire run without a safety net. The end of the run went just as smoothly. The skids were deployed, and the bike was brought to rest upright and with ease. We were honing our skills and becoming more confident in the little things.

When we finally packed up to head back home, we left with a feeling of accomplishment. The crew worked well together. We learned about towing. We learned about balance and the capabilities of the skids. We learned about not giving up. But we *didn't* learn a damn thing about parachutes!

Yet . . .

Chapter Four
Running With the Big Boys

After several weeks back home, we once again packed our bags and headed to the salt. Denis had inked a deal with Craig Breedlove, who was scheduled to test his jet-powered car during the same week. Sharing the salt on private time cut our expenses in half. We each had our own course. Ours was about 7 miles in length. Breedlove's was over 10. Being strapped to a jet engine capable of breaking the speed of sound required a little extra room, mostly for stopping. Eventually we would be running on a course of equal length, but it wouldn't be on this trip.

Buddy, my brother, "sticking it" to Harley-Davidson's million-dollar man Jay Springsteen during the Grand National season opener. *Photo courtesy of Dan Mahony*

Pulling into the pits, it was obvious the Breedlove camp was playing hardball. They had assembled a giant white tent that was practically as big as our entire shop back home. His truck and trailer rig was state of the art. Fancy paint, lots of chrome, and deep-pocketed sponsors fought for position along the side of the big, enclosed trailer. A life-size mural of his famous car was also painted on the side.

His team seemed to have it all: a talented crew in matching uniforms, tons of tools, even a chef and a masseuse. *And* they had great toys. I'll get into that later.

They also brought the press. Speedvision was probably the biggest headliner, but several other forms of media were there, including a reporter from *Penthouse* magazine.

For being the new kids on the block, we didn't do too bad ourselves. We showed up with a decent following of family and friends to cheer us on. We also had a few things the big corporate racing team did not. To our credit, we had air superiority. My dad and brother both flew private airplanes. We invited them along to sort of monitor the course from a bird's-eye view.

To set the stage, I have to take you back to the previous night at the Stateline Inn. The crew congregated around Shooters, the local watering hole, waiting for the rest of the team to arrive. We had just finished an eight-hour drive through the desert, so the plan was to adjourn to our rooms for a quick shower before meeting up for dinner in the Bonneville Room to discuss strategies.

As I mentioned earlier, at the time I was recently divorced and living a sort of haphazard lifestyle. I was in my early 30s, and had a new girlfriend who was all of 22. She was a beautiful redhead, as fast and dangerous as any racing machine ever made. At that point in my life she was just what the doctor ordered. Her name was Kelly, but we all remember her as *Squeaky,* due to her high-pitched voice.

Anyway, about the time we were all headed for our rooms for a quick rinse, my brother, my mom, and Squeaky all show up at the receptionist's desk. They had just flown in to the Wendover Airport. (Wendover is home to the *Enola Gay*, the plane that dropped the bomb on Hiroshima.) I'm excited, my crew's impressed, and Denis is worried. Everyone exchanges greetings and departs for their rooms. Denis corners Squeaky and warns her to go easy on me. "The lad needs his rest. We got a big day tomorrow, you know." She smiles innocently, batting her big green eyes. Denis shakes his head and smiles. He points his finger at me as if to warn me, too, but only smiles wider. He pats me on the back and reminds me we have a dinner meeting in about 30 minutes.

Squeaky and I dart off to our room. Needless to say, we ran a little late making it to the party . . .

* * *

The Spirit of America and its driver were both legends in their own right. A little over 30 years ago Craig Breedlove, driving a jet-powered car with that name, was the first to break 600 mph. He did it right here at Bonneville. At the end of his return run, the parachutes failed and he ended up snapping off a couple of telephone poles before ramping off the levee and finally crash-landing nose first into salty water on the other side. He was luckily able to walk away unhurt. As for the jet-powered car, I'm sure extra attention would be taken next time in the area of the parachutes and the brakes—just my opinion . . .

* * *

The day started early. We were pulling onto the salt just as the sun was rising. It's hard to describe the beauty of it all. The sky was on fire: reds, yellows, different shades of orange. The reflection against the vast white floor was amazing. In sharp contrast, the stale coffee from the 24-hour gas station was the worst you could buy anywhere. When you're hundreds of miles away from home, you learn to take the good with the bad.

My brother Buddy had brought along a video camera to film the event to take back home. Some of the footage shot from his plane shows just how fast we are capable of going. He flies a Cessna 210 with retractable landing gear—not a slow airplane. In the footage, you can see the streamliner catch and pass him from the ground, and leave him trailing helplessly behind. He also filmed the sunrise, but seeing it on film does not do it justice.

The Breedlove camp was running late. While we were opening up shop, high on week-old coffee, they were sleeping in, or maybe running on Utah time. Either way, it gave us a chance to focus on the job at hand without any distractions.

Appropriate changes were made to allow for a new starter design that connected on the opposite side of the motor. To deal with the cold morning air, our commercial-sized 40-cup coffee pot had been sacrificed as an oil heater. The engine oil was drained and poured into the large, aluminum tub and plugged in. None of us dared, but I'm sure if we tried it, it couldn't have tasted much worse than the stuff we were drinking.

When it had reached a suitable temperature, it was poured back in the motor and made ready to fire. The sun was barely overhead when we brought *Medusa* to life.

That moment gave me goose bumps. The sky was a colorful orange hue. The crisp morning air kept the crew huddled close together while John coupled the starter motor to the end of the crank and pulled the trigger. After a few reluctant turns, the ignition fired and *Medusa* roared to life. The hair on the back of my neck stood up as the angry growl echoed down the salt. Denis revved it a few times, and left it to cackle at idle. There wasn't a face within a hundred yards that didn't have a smile on it.

I took my turn at the controls, blipping the throttle and watching the MoTeC screen. Even in warmup mode, *Medusa* was serious business. Imagine 420 horsepower at your fingertips—in a motorcycle! The power-to-weight ratio is staggering. I was a bit nervous, but totally excited. My brother grabbed his camera to record the sound. He was just as excited, if not more.

About the time the show ended, a new one was about to begin. *Medusa's* fire was taken away, bringing the vast expanse of Bonneville back to a calm, silent arena. A faint noise hummed, off in the distance. It slowly became louder and more distinguishable. A small dot appeared in the sky, and grew larger as the hum became louder.

Pitting behind the levee wall, we lost the dot behind the embankment. Moments later a tremendous roar blared overhead as half our crew ducked for cover. A blue and white airplane cleared the levee by not more than a couple of feet. He buzzed the pits and our crew, flying dangerously low and at full throttle. Enter Joe, my dad, pushing the limits of his Bellanca 260 *Cardboard Connie*, just as was expected of me when I had my turn behind the wheel.

It sort of ran in our family. My dad is still the most fearless man I've ever known. My brother is a close second. My dad raced motorcycles when Triumphs and BSAs were considered *good handling* dirt bikes. He flew airplanes like they were an extension of himself. He also scared the hell out of me. To this day I'm still uncomfortable flying.

My brother also flew with the same carefree attitude—afraid of nothing. In the early 1980s my brother raced the Camel Pro series on mile and half-mile ovals like myself. But it was on the big TT tracks of the same series where he really shined. He didn't have the factory equipment of the highly paid top riders of the time. But on the TT track he didn't need it.

A large black-and-white framed picture still hangs proudly on the wall of his garage that says it all. Jay Springsteen was the Grand National Champion, riding for the Harley-Davidson factory. The big Number One was proudly displayed on the front of his bike. The race was at the Houston Astrodome, the season opener for the

Grand National series. Both Jay and my brother struggled through their heat races and had one last chance in the semi to make it through to the main event.

Jay Springsteen was the hands-down favorite to win the semi. Hell, he was the favorite to win the whole thing. My brother, on the other hand, had nothing to lose. In those days he was called the Bud Man because he was sponsored by Budweiser beer. They liked his style and bravado, even though he was a definite underdog to the likes of a full factory-sponsored rider. The funny thing was, nothing intimidated him. Nothing . . .

At the start of the race, the flag dropped and the pack fought for position before entering the first turn. As they hit the enormous, hard-packed dirt jump that followed, the champ was up front with my brother about four bike lengths behind.

Springer hurled his big XR 750 into the air, confident no one was able to push the envelope as hard as he. The Bud Man gained two or three bike lengths on the champ before they hit the ground! He flew so high through the air that when he landed, the bike bounced another 3 or 4 feet off the ground before gravity finally wrestled him back to earth. He had such a tremendous drive going that he decided to make his move on the champ before they entered the tight right-hander that was fast approaching. The photo was taken at exactly the right moment when contact was made. My brother had stuffed the big bucks factory rider so hard that the champ high-sided before reaching the apex of the turn. The frozen moment shows Springer's eyes bulging with panic as the big XR prepares to be pummeled into the ground. His leg is outstretched, his body contorted and out of control. My brother's front wheel is buried inside the factory race machine, pushing it out from under the champ like yesterday's garbage.

The champ was down, and my brother was in the main event. And now he and my dad were here at Bonneville to support me trying to go fast in a straight line by myself. It's a tough act to follow, but even they are impressed with what we are doing. I'll be damned if I'm going to let them down.

So after a couple of high-speed, low-altitude fly-bys, my dad touches gently down on the salt and taxis into our pit. He and his close friend, Bonnie, climb out onto the wing and survey the moon-like setting. Moments later, greetings are exchanged and my dad and Bonnie get the nickel tour of our operation. For a dollar more, he coaxes us to take him over to the Breedlove camp so he can catch a glimpse of the new jet-car. For a guy who has flown antique airplanes most of his life, seeing the *Spirit of America* firsthand is a pretty impressive sight.

Corporate Racing was finally awake, as evidenced by the long caravan of vehicles finally making their way into the Breedlove pit to punch in and get to work. Their uniforms were neatly pressed and their fingernails were free from the grime one might expect from your typical, everyday mechanic. The coffee was hot, and the bagels and doughnuts were fresh. Corporate Racing was quite *civilized.* I tossed my day-old, gas station java in their immaculate receptacle and helped myself to a cup of Starbucks' finest.

At Bonneville, the clock is always ticking. After we finished making the rounds and checking out all the cool stuff that oil companies and television sports stations could buy, it was time to get our own dog and pony act in gear. We politely excused ourselves and headed back to the cheap seats, where we would spend the next two days trying to prove to ourselves and anyone else who cared to watch, that we had what it takes to go fast.

All kidding aside, Craig Breedlove is a class act and one hell of a nice man. His talent shows in the craftsmanship and beauty of his race machine. His record speaks for itself. And the fact that, at 60 years old, he's still got more balls than a driving range left a lasting impression on my mind . . .

Bonnie and my dad offer to take my brother back to the airport so he can bring his own plane out to the salt to join in the festivities. While they are away, we gear up for our first run of the day. The plan is to make our first motorized pass in first gear. If it handles okay under power, the next run will be different.

The bike is fired, the tow vehicle takes me up to 65, and I release. I roll on the throttle and am instantly reassured that the bike is easier to handle with the rotating mass of the heavy flywheels. Life is good. I steadily increase the rpm while watching the speedometer climb. It's amazing how easy the bike accelerates. It *likes* it. I'm liking it, too. When the speedometer hits 165, I roll out of it. The tach has nearly reached redline, so our job is done.

I wasn't going quite fast enough to get the full effect of the parachutes, but I hit them anyway. The high-speed chute did little to impress me, putting a slight drag from behind. I deployed one of the main chutes and for the first time, I got to feel the power of airbrakes. It wasn't anything earth-shattering, but it did slow the bike down substantially in a rather short distance. Once below a certain speed, though, the effect was all but gone. From there I had to rely on "old faithful" to bring me the rest of the way down. It took a while, but eventually it stopped.

No sooner had I released my harness and lifted the canopy, than two of the lowest flying high-speed airplanes I ever saw buzzed me from directly behind. They were so low I could actually feel the wind they were pushing blow by me, kicking up wafts of salt. The two metal birds then pointed upward and raced out of sight. My brother and my dad were back . . .

Denis was the first to my side and wanted to know how it went. I guess my smile said it all. I briefed him on everything, and told him how much easier it was to control under power. He asked how I liked the parachutes. He knew *eventually* I would come around. "They were pretty good, I guess." I still wasn't prepared to admit I didn't need *"no stinking brakes"* . . . not yet.

The one thing I did learn about parachutes is that they can be a bitch to repack. That was my job, and my job only. When the time came that it really mattered for the parachutes to work, it would be my own responsibility. This was not a job to be taken lightly.

When we got back to the pits, Denis showed me a couple of different ways to pack a parachute. It would be my decision as to which way I wanted it done and which way I felt more comfortable with—which way I thought would save my ass in the event of an emergency. Reality was finally starting to set in. These parachutes were the one thing that could save my life.

I learned to pack them quickly, but most importantly I learned to pack them right. It was about a 15-minute job per parachute—and there would always be at least two of them to repack. They had to be laid out flat and all the cumulative salt shaken free. The nylon lanyard that attached the ropes to the parachutes had to be inspected for abrasions and tears after every use. Same with the chutes themselves.

The saving grace was that my mom and Squeaky had shown up. Mom brought munchies, and Squeaky brought smiles and grins. Come to think of it, after everyone tasted my mom's cooking, she got her fair share of those, too. I put Squeaky to work helping me pack the chutes and not long after, we were ready for our next run.

This time we would be running her through all four gears. Nothing crazy, just make sure she shifts correctly and handles comfortably at speed. Denis reminded me we were on a short course and that once we started going faster, it would take more room to get stopped. He also reminded me that the parachutes would react much harsher at high speed, and to be prepared. *Yeah, yeah, yeah. I've heard this one before . . .*

The Breedlove crew was still hard at it, preparing everything for their first test run of the day. As luck would have it, we were ready first and decided to give it another go. Before preparing to fire off the bike, Denis gathered the crew and had a little pow-wow about safety concerns and other important issues that I usually try not to dwell on.

The meeting drew a pretty good crowd, including the medical technicians, many of the waiting press from corporate racing, and Craig Breedlove's pet dog, Midnight. It was a serious meeting, and for the first time in my brief land-speed-racing career, I was feeling a little anxious about what was about to happen next. My girlfriend started turning a little pale, and even shed a tear that exposed itself once it ran past the base of her sunglasses. My mom stepped in to comfort her and, sure enough, the tears started running from her eyes as well.

The scorecard read as follows: My dad was ready for some excitement. My brother was excited, but understandably concerned. Denis was stoked—he was living his dream. I was excited, but had a minor case of butterflies. (Nothing I couldn't handle though.) The crew was tentatively excited. They wanted to go fast, but not *too* fast, yet. They wanted more proof that everything was going to work. The press showed interest. My mom and Squeaky showed utter terror. Craig Breedlove showed enthusiasm, and his dog . . . well, he hunched over and crapped right in front of us! It was a perfect ending to a serious moment. We all had a good laugh and went back to the business at hand of preparing to go fast.

The crew dispersed to various sections along the course, waiting to see firsthand if *Tenacious II* was worth its salt. My dad and brother went airborne and circled the area to make sure the strip was clear. John deployed the starter, which made some rather unusual noises as it strained and clattered, but finally brought the sleeping giant back to life.

This was it. I was going to finally see what it was like to go fast. Maybe not quite full out, but faster than ever before. John gave me the thumbs up and jumped in the tow vehicle next to Vern. I revved the motor and it screamed like a Formula One race car engine ready to be let loose on the pavement. My heartbeat joined the race and was now pounding in unison with the motor.

At 20 mph the skids were up and I was ready to go. Sixty-five couldn't come fast enough. When the speedo hit the mark I released the strap and did a slingshot by the right side of Vern and John. I buried my helmet into the top of the roll cage and twisted the throttle as far as my wrist could physically turn. My fingers crawled forward on the grip until the throttle was pinned.

When I hit second gear it was the biggest rush I ever experienced. I was pushed back in my seat in the same way a passenger of a jet airliner sinks in the back of his seat during takeoff. The acceleration was amazing. I went from 165 to 240 mph all in second gear! At one point the rear wheel broke loose and started to spin. The rpm climbed, but the wheels remained in line. This was the first time I'd ever driven anything that could light up the rear tire and keep going perfectly straight! It didn't drift an inch off line . . .

When I went for third, it missed the gear and went into neutral. "Holy shit!" was the first thought that crossed my mind. I hit the button a second time after the revs had died down, and this time the tranny god was smiling. I had lost some momentum and had to bring her back up to speed from about 225 mph. Third gear carried me to about 260. Third would have carried me farther, but because of the missed shift I was beginning to run out of room and still wanted to make sure we tried all four gears before throwing out the laundry.

A strange thing happened once I inched past about 240 mph. Up to that point, it felt just like you would probably imagine. I mean, we were hauling ass, and that's pretty much just what it felt like. But after that, a lot of strange little things start to happen.

First off, your vision starts to blur uncontrollably. The frequency of the vibrations are working faster than the reflexes of the muscles in your eyes that allow them to maintain focus. You can see the contrasts of the groomed salt of the racecourse versus the darker, ungroomed surface to either side. The mile markers become harder to make out, and they seem to be stacking up, one behind the other.

Another interesting bit of information is the way the bike handles at high speed. At about 240, the aerodynamics of the machine become very critical. Where before I was jamming along, countersteering to maintain proper balance and to stay centered in the middle of the course (without much difficulty), now I'm flying an airplane that has no wings . . . and is supposed to be flown on the ground.

Steering and balance become much more intense. Every move I make no longer only affects the tiny contact patch where rubber meets salt. Now I have to counter the airflow that is squeezing tightly against our fish-shaped fiberglass body. It doesn't like sudden changes. In fact, it really doesn't like any changes at all. Having said that, it still has the surface area of a streamlined, mini-Winnebago. Side winds at these speeds can cause instant gray hairs and sphincter retractions that were thought humanly impossible. You have to react calmly, but forcefully. Now is the time when man and machine have to have an understanding of who's the boss. This is what land speed racing is all about . . .

I make the shift to fourth cleanly. I'm now going faster than all but a small handful of folks have ever gone on two wheels. At this point I'm admittedly concerned about my immediate safety. At some point I'm going to have to slow this locomotive down, but for now, it's all I can do to keep the throttle twisted and stay between the lines. The wind slowly eases me to the far side of the track, and I'm not too sure I can keep her between the lines much longer.

I sail through the measured mile at a little over 280 mph. I've had more than enough excitement already, and I'm ready to drop anchor and bring this thing back to within the legal speed limit.

I wish it were as easy as that.

I fight to bring the bike as close to the center of the course as I can, stand her on her toes, and release the high-speed chute. I leave the throttle wide open until I feel a tug from behind, then roll steadily out of the throttle. The reason for this is weight transfer. If I were to just chop the throttle and wait for the parachute to open, the weight would shift to the front of the bike and overload the front end. This could result in a tire failure, possible loss of control due to the rear end trying to come around and pass the front, or maybe nothing at all. I wasn't going to wait around to find out.

I glance at the speedometer and notice the tiny 18-inch chute is slowing the bike down, but it's about as efficient as Denis's rear disc brake that I'm always complaining about. No, I want to stop now. I brace myself and squeeze the button that releases the main parachute.

Okay, so maybe *Denis was right* . . .

When the main parachute finally opened (remember, I'm traveling at quite a high rate of speed, and it takes a little while for this whole "air brake" thing to happen), I thought I was literally going to be thrown through the front of the motorcycle and probably run over by it before the whole ordeal was over.

It slowed down so fast that my restraints actually embedded into my body. I felt like my body would squirt right out the neck hole of my racing suit like a cartoon character. And once the parachute was deployed, it stayed deployed. It wasn't like I could just take my foot off the brakes! My head was tossed forward, my eyes were probably closed, and for a brief moment I was no longer the driver, I was just along for the ride. And what a ride it was . . .

I glanced at the speedometer as I regained control of the machine. The numbers were dropping faster than the prices on a Wal-Mart commercial. I disengaged the transmission and freewheeled while I fumbled around trying to find the ignition cutoff. Visibility is somewhat limited in the cockpit due to my ride angle and the mandatory neck brace. I can't really see below the Plexiglas windshield, but I have everything pretty well memorized.

I cut the engine and coast down to somewhere below 80 mph and start easing on the rear disc brake. It is only then that I realize the significance of what Denis has been telling me all along. The brakes are a mere novelty when traveling at speeds nearing 300 mph. They would overheat in an instant and become useless were you to actually engage them at speed. The braking force of a ribboned, six-foot chute is incredible. It was then and there that I became a believer.

* * *

It's amazing how your world can change in the blink of an eye. Before that run I was just another wannabe who liked to go fast on a motorcycle. After that pass (thanks to Denis and our entire crew) I was one of the four fastest men to ever twist a throttle on a motorcycle. This dream of one day being the world's fastest was starting to become a reality. Maybe not now, maybe not for another couple of years (we still had to gain almost 50 more mph), but from that point on we knew it was within our reach.

"Corporate Racing" was finally ready to burn a hot lap when we returned. The beautiful jet car was towed in place at the edge of the strip and readied for action. Breedlove's entourage was quite impressive. His color-coordinated crew hovered around him and his machine like he was royalty. The press shoved cameras and microphones in front of and into anything that made noise or shined. Our own crew had temporarily abandoned the world of two wheels and piston power, and joined the show of jet propulsion and technology beyond comprehension. In a nutshell, it was great.

The sound coming from this futuristic desert racer seemed more at home at an airport than on the salt. As the jet turbine's rpm increased, the high-pitched whine became steadily higher and louder. After nearly 30 minutes of last-minute preparations, Craig Breedlove and the *Spirit of America* inched slowly forward.

As he pulled away, the sound became deeper and louder still. He began to pick up speed, *but nothing to write home about.* After he was nearly a mile away, the afterburner kicked in for only a brief moment.

But that's all it took.

The sound was so powerful, so deep . . . it literally shook the ground. Its heavy bass tone reverberated inside of you. It was harnessed thunder, scarier than hell, yet equally seductive. The crowd fell silent as we watched this phallic-like shape barrel down the salt. Dark clouds of smoke billowed from behind, signaling all was not well. His army of followers jumped in their rented cars and minivans and gave chase to their hero.

Truth be told, on this day, two wheels and piston power had top speed of the meet. We had a lot to be happy about. But tomorrow would be another day . . .

* * *

The sun came up, just as it always does, but today things would not be the same. Not for us, nor for Breedlove and company. The stakes were getting higher. For Breedlove, corporate money and incentive-based contracts were on the line. Not to mention the fact that his legion of fans and paparazzi had not yet witnessed what they had come to see.

On our end, yesterday we cleared 280. It was a thrilling experience for our entire crew. We didn't have the multimillion dollar contracts on the table. We didn't have the paparazzi watching our every move with cameras rolling and notebooks in hand. (Not yet, anyway.) What we *did* have was tenacity. We were here for the long haul. Money or no money, we knew we would keep coming back until the record was ours. Our enthusiasm was contagious. It showed that morning when the press wandered over to "Club BUB" to hang out and have a closer look.

Right from the get-go we found the day would not be an easy one. The starter motor self-destructed while we were attempting to fire the engine before the first run. John disemboweled the external starter motor and discovered the problem to be terminal. The official time of death was somewhere around 8 a.m. A brief ceremony of *oh shits* and *oh fucks* immediately followed. The press was quick to lose interest, and soon found themselves sauntering back to Corporate Racing for free refills of hot Starbucks and fresh bagels.

We assembled a quick meeting to discuss our options. Being an ex flat track racer, I thought bump starting the bike was the only logical choice, and everyone seemed to agree. We rigged the tow strap and dragged the bike up to speed. I dumped the clutch, thinking the rear wheel would turn over the motor and we'd have a runner in no time.

As it turned out, when I let out the clutch, the engine locked under compression and skidded the rear wheel. The tow strap tore from the release and I was left stranded about 100 yards outside of the pits with a dead motor. *Medusa* had too much compression to bump start in first gear. After a few more failed attempts, we were finally able to breathe life into the stubborn beast at a higher tow speed in a taller gear.

Problem solved. It was time to go racing . . .

While we were gearing up, Corporate Racing had readied themselves for an early morning run. They had actually beaten us to the starting grid due to our previously mentioned mechanical failure. We watched in awe as the master of speed once again inched away from the starting grid. This time the smoke spewed even earlier, but nonetheless, he made his run, logging another test run into the books.

His misfortune turned into opportunity for "Club BUB." How many chances do you get to outrun a jet-powered racer capable of breaking the speed of sound? Well, it seemed we had at least one more . . .

Tires play a big part in almost any kind of high-speed racing. Breedlove's jet car doesn't even use rubber. He runs a specially designed Kevlar material wrapped around huge, aluminum rims. It seems there isn't a rubber compound designed yet to handle the kinds of speeds he hopes to achieve.

As for us, we still ran good ol' Goodyear rubber on our machine. We had tires specifically designed for land-speed record (LSR) racing. Maybe not exactly for motorcycle use, but if it's good enough to be run on all fours in excess of 300 mph, it was good enough for us to try on two.

Or so we thought . . .

Our next pass was a real learning experience. We knew it was time to take it to the next level. It was no longer good enough to go 280 mph. Denis and I had a long talk about all the possibilities. Somehow he must have sensed I was a little nervous—at least, I *think* that was his reasoning for the terrible, terrible thing he would soon do.

After our last-minute briefing, he sent the crew off in different directions to man their posts for the next run. John and Jeff Boyle stayed behind to connect me to the tow vehicle and make sure all systems were go.

Denis, who usually takes off early and heads for the far end of the course, decided to sway from his normal routine. Just as John and Jeff had finished adjusting my harness and securing the tow strap, Denis intervened for some final words of wisdom. "Are you ready, laddie?" he asked with a shit-eating grin.

"I guess so." I looked up at him, wondering what he was still doing hanging around. "Everything okay?" I asked.

"Perfect. Everything's puss." His smile widened as he stared at me as if waiting for some sort of response.

That's when it hit me.

In an instant the canopy was slammed shut and the latch

engaged. A tear came to my eye at just the thought of what he had done. He signaled the tow vehicle to take up the slack and get the show under way. I also heard him laugh. The bastard . . .

What he had done was break wind in a *very* large way. We're talking more volatile than nitrous. And once he did, he latched it inside with me! I was trapped and held captive! All I wanted to do was go, go, go . . . There's not a lot of airflow in the cockpit so his memory was with me for most of that run.

Once under way, I accelerated harder and faster than ever before. The rear tire broke loose in second gear and left a dark trail of burnt rubber for more than a mile and a half! (We measured it after the run.) It was "no drama," as they say in Australia, as the bike went straight as an arrow. The run was our fastest yet, at 291 mph. I can't begin to describe how it felt. I was so happy—so alive . . .

I was met at the far end of the track by reporters, cameramen (and women), and my family and friends. I had a good luck charm from my girlfriend that I had stuffed into my pocket before the run. Before crawling out of the cramped quarters in the cockpit, I took it out and hung it on the handlebars. (It was black and silky, and not much larger than an unraveled roll of dental floss.) Nobody seemed to notice, but I'll bet they caught it on tape as they filmed me climbing from the machine. *I'm sure Squeaky will never tell* . . .

Denis shook my hand and congratulated me on a fantastic run. I told him he was one smelly son of a bitch. We had a good laugh but it took a while for it to sink in what was really going on. He knew that I was nervous about never before going at such high speed. Not everyone walks away from a crash going that fast. What he had done, in his own twisted way, was take my mind off my worries completely. I was relaxed and only wanted to get going and get some air circulating. I guess his little trick worked . . . (What a bad, bad, man . . .)

Chapter Five
"Houston, We Have a Problem"

Upon further inspection after the run, we learned of a couple of problems. The first was that we destroyed the rear tire during the last run. Large pieces of rubber had chunked away from the massive carcass, leaving deep, jagged holes in the damaged tread. Excessive wheelspin was to blame.

Fixing the problem wouldn't be an easy task. We still needed to go faster. The tires would be pushed harder as our speeds increased. The short-term fix was to replace the tire. We had another run to make.

One of the benefits of having a fairly open-minded crew was their willingness to try new things. Bob Lobenburg, a race consultant and

My brother Buddy in the pilot's seat. *Photo courtesy of Ed Chamberlain*

former Trans Am racer, came along as part of a package deal we had going with the installation of our new data retrieval system. He offered some advice on adjusting the suspension to make the bike more neutral. Doing this involved taking some preload out of the front end, which would essentially "soften" the ride up front.

From the beginning I was very skeptical. The bike handled fine, and it was pretty stable at speed. I didn't want to lose that. My brother and my dad (both ex-motorcycle racers), agreed with my opinion. "If it ain't broke, don't *fuck* with it." Words of wisdom from my dad.

Denis was undecided. I don't think he was too crazy about the idea, but Bob talked him into it. It was a compromise. We didn't have the right spring rate available, so we backed off the preload. Bob wanted three turns. I didn't want any. Denis settled on one turn, or so he said.

It was a bad decision no matter how many turns they ended up using.

The next pass almost put an early end to our racing effort. With new rubber on the back and a softer front end suspension setting, we set out to up the ante. The bike accelerated hard, the rear tire once again starting to spin. I did my best to save the tire, but hey, we were in a hurry. We went through the paces and soon enough we were in fourth gear looking to put our team on the map.

That's when things got ugly.

At about 270 mph, the bike started to weave slightly. The rear tire being in a constant drift didn't help matters either. I tried to counter each weave, but it progressively got worse. I suddenly realized what was going on. With the front suspension on the softer setting, the aerodynamic load on the front end was overcoming the spring and forcing the front suspension to collapse. As the nose of the bike lowered, an even greater force was created.

Now the front tire was becoming severely overloaded—far past its intended safety margin. We would later learn that the tire itself was collapsing inward, causing the front end to behave erratically. On occasion, the spring would rebound, forcing the front end back up, only to be quickly overcome and forced back into its originally overloaded state.

This caused a sort of slow-motion high-speed wobble. All I knew was things were starting to get out of hand. I had to make a decision as to whether or not I should abort the run. I was already approaching 280 mph and the measured mile was coming into sight. You only get so many chances to run at these speeds, and each attempt may be your last. I was still upright and traveling in a generally forward direction. I decided to ride it out and hope for the best.

I countered and weaved all the way through the measured mile. Top speed for the run was a disappointing 286 mph. The bike handled so poorly that when it came time to hit the parachutes I was afraid something might let go. I had no choice but to throw out the laundry and hope this nightmare would come to an end. I'd used up so much room trying to get the bike straight before dropping anchor that there was little room left for stopping.

Once the first big chute had deployed and its mighty jolt was over, I released the backup chute, which put a major *whoa* on everything. Up until this point I'd never opened more than one of the main chutes after a run. But up until now, I'd never wanted the ride to be over so quickly. I wanted out, pronto.

When Denis asked me what happened, I was less than cordial. Pissed would be a better description. I told him all about the run, and how it almost got away from me at high speed. I also told him my views on his and Lobenburg's suspension changes. I was a little hot, and probably overreacted a bit, but it was my ass on the line and I just wanted to make sure the message was coming across loud and clear.

After all the data was downloaded, they were better able to appreciate what I had been through. They played the run over and over, impressed that we made it through the lights at all. After I had a chance to cool down I apologized for my rudeness. Everyone was just doing their jobs. Having altered the suspension settings gave us a better understanding of what was really going on. It helped us make the right decision to go to a heavier-duty tire for future runs that probably saved our ass. All in all, the experience ended on a positive note . . .

* * *

Some people compare themselves with others by how much money they make. For others, it may be how they live, or how their family life is. For women (at least for some) it may be their clothes or their husband's success. But for this particular group, it's much more primal than that. We judge one another by what is most important to any man—his toys.

Here's proof that boys never really grow up. *They just get better toys.*

During one of the many breaks in the hot sun on the great white plains, the Breedlove camp was the first to come out and play. Now I always bring something along to help pass the time away. A unicycle, my Gas Gas trials bike (you'd be amazed how far you can wheelie when there's nothing to hit for miles), bicycles, or even an occasional dirt bike or go kart.

Corporate Racing held their own when it came to cool toys. We were all sitting around while our race machines were being attended to when we heard this loud, thunderous howl coming from just in front of the Breedlove pits. A crowd had gathered to watch as this go kart came flying onto the salt at a fairly high rate of speed.

This wasn't your average, run-of-the-mill, Briggs and Stratton special. These boys raced a jet-powered car so, naturally, they had to have a jet-powered go kart as well. I kid you not. This thing was rigged with a propane powered pulse-jet motor! There was a huge, cone-shaped exhaust pointing up into the air. The driver of the kart kept one hand on the steering wheel, and the other on this large valve. When he opened the valve, it fed fuel into the flame, which pushed the kart along at a very impressive clip. The sound it made was enormous. A deafening howl bellowed out of the stack when the valve was open, and except for the tiny rubber tires crunching across the salt, near silence was all that was heard when the valve was closed again, allowing the driver to make a turn.

There was no throttle control to speak of, just on or off, depending on whether the valve was open or closed. It made the ride that much more exciting. Pretty cool stuff.

At the end of the day, it was our turn to display a few toys of our own. Being that we were on the piston-power team, it was almost a given that we would have a piston-powered toy of some kind.

Ingenuity ran high in both camps when it came time to play. But as Denis would always say, "We may not win every race, but we never lose a party." With that, our two-stroke, gas-motor-powered, straight-pipe-equipped margarita machine was removed from its padded carrying case and brought to the table. Howard Carte, our very own *party test pilot,* did the honors of bringing the former weed-whacker motor turned "super blender" to life.

Running on two-cycle racing fuel with a splash of methanol, the tiny motor screamed at the top of its lungs as ice and tequila, along with a splash of that green stuff, was whipped into a frothy, high-octane cocktail. Our cups were moistened around the rims, and then ground into the salty surface we were standing on. The high-pitched whine coming from the straight pipe of our culinary contraption beckoned those from our neighboring pit to come by and share in the festivities. Many a brain freeze was recorded in the moments to come as the frothy contents were choked down at a pace not recommended by the Surgeon General.

And then there were the fireworks.

Boys and their toys . . . let's face it. A jet-powered race car that is damn near capable of breaking the speed of sound? A streamlined motorcycle designed to travel well over 300 mph? These are nothing more than extreme toys. This is what makes life so great for some of us. But there's another favorite pastime for most boys (young and old) that, up until now, hasn't been mentioned. We all love blowing things up. The bigger the boom, the better!

For some unknown reason, Bonneville racers seem to be well connected in the pyrotechnics industry. We've all played with bottle rockets and firecrackers in our youth, but out on the salt flats, that's where the heavy artillery is displayed. Without going into too much detail, I will say that on more than one occasion we have deployed mortars in excess of four inches in diameter! Where they came from isn't what's important. The sheer magnitude of the explosion is what counts. The fact that an anonymous, misguided individual actually launched one into the sky just over the methanol racing-fuel truck and pit area, will not be discussed here. As was stated earlier, "We might not win every race, but we never lose a party!" Such is the life of a racer . . .

When it was time for my dad to leave, we anticipated his signature, low-altitude fly-by and lined up across the salt, forming a seven-moon salute. You heard correctly. Seven able-bodied grown men hunched over with their pants pulled down below their knees, mooning a fast approaching airplane.

As we're all lined up there on the salt, seven foolish souls of various shapes and sizes, it suddenly occurred to some that Joe Robinson was flying so low that they were actually looking *down* at him. This would tend to leave a somewhat vulnerable feeling, considering our current state.

As he roared ever closer, the nose of the plane held steady, not lifting in the least. We were about to play a 200-mile-per-hour game of chicken! Well, I for one knew my dad wouldn't actually hit anybody. I wasn't moving. Denis, on the other hand, must have decided that since he was the biggest target, he would be the first to go. You haven't lived until you've seen a very large man with his pants tangled around his ankles, trying to sprint to the sidelines with his bare ass in the air and his knuckles dragging on the salt for balance! *Not a pretty picture, actually.*

As my dad neared his target, he pulled up at the last possible moment, just clearing us, and more importantly, just clearing the salty embankment we had pitted in front of. The sound of a fire-walled motor only a few feet overhead, was definitely a nerve-racking experience. Watching him just barely escape over the top of the levee was insane . . . and some people think *I'm* crazy . . .

Packing up to head back home and once again face our day jobs, we knew we had our work cut out for us. The bike was fast and handled fairly well, but there were still some pretty serious problems that needed to be sorted out. Wheelspin at speed was definitely one of them. The transmission still needed work, and the front tire proved to be borderline at best.

Changes would be made and we'd be back. Tenacity was the very foundation of our team. We'd find better tires. The transmission would be tweaked some more for better reliability. Different suspension settings would be introduced. And when we returned, our toy would be better than it had ever been before . . .

Chapter Six
The Determining Factor

S ooner or later you have to decide whether you've done everything you can or if there's still something else you haven't tried that might bring you success. For us, that decision came after our final visit to Bonneville with *Tenacious II* in the fall of 1999.

We'd now made the trek from the foothills to the salt on a number of occasions. Private time, officially sanctioned meets, and even our own "motorcycles only" meet all turned out basically the same results—291 was our best number. We'd made many improvements to the bike over time, but none that actually tacked on miles per hour. It handled better. The tires lasted

Off to a wet start at Bonneville. *Photo courtesy of Gene Koch*

longer. The starter gremlins went away. Even the transmission was getting better.

In our own defense, there were actually a few things working *against* us. The famed Bonneville Salt Flats oddly enough, was one. During the late 1990s, the smooth, hard surface had begun to deteriorate to a point where a committee was actually formed to try and save the salt. All the years of strip-mining the salt flats of its rich minerals had come at a price. The salt was wearing thin, and was no longer ideal for speed racing, especially of the two-wheeled variety.

The committee developed a plan that would eventually turn things around for the great salt plains. At the end of each year, the recovered brine would be pumped back onto the salt flats. It would take many years to restore, but it was a project worth pursuing. Racing could continue, and the famed Bonneville Salt Flats would eventually be rejuvenated.

When we came to Bonneville for the last time in the fall of 1999 we were nearing the end of our rope with *Tenacious II*. The sponsors had been great, the crew had done everything possible to keep things rolling, and Denis and John were now spending all of their free time trying to make *Tenacious II* faster.

The front wheel and tire had been replaced with a beefier carcass riding on a custom wheel made by Precision Machine. Aerodynamic discs were attached to the sides for less drag. The rear tire had most of the tread removed for less heat and rubber fatigue. The exhaust outlets that exited the spent gases directly overhead were now repositioned so as not to upset airflow against the rear of the bodywork. This minor change was responsible for keeping the rear of the bike pressurized, and not allowing it to "lift" at speed. Tire life and wheelspin were dramatically improved by this change alone.

Air scoops were added to the sides of the bike just behind the windshield to feed the engine more air. This problem became obvious the faster we went. The air would blow past the original air vents, buffeting off the windshield and creating a void where it was originally intended to go.

As mentioned earlier, this event and the circumstances surrounding it brought about an unlikely decision. We had made a few passes earlier on in the day. All the changes we had made to the bike seemed to be for the better. The downside was the course was in pretty bad shape and the wind was not too forgiving on this particular day. Add to that the fact that the moisture in the salt was slowly coming to the surface, and you could see what kind of day we were having.

To make matters worse, it was the end of the season. This would be our last run of the year. Winter would soon be upon us and the famed Bonneville Salt Flats would once again be submerged, transforming the hard, slick racing surface into a salty quagmire at best. This would ultimately turn out to be our last racing effort for *Tenacious II* on American soil.

I remember the run like it was yesterday. The late afternoon sun was beaming overhead. The far end of the course had standing water on it that began right at the end of the measured mile. We struggled with conditions all day and the whole crew's patience was wearing thin. We needed that one perfect pass to make things right. We only had time for one more run, but sometimes that could make all the difference.

Denis and I spoke briefly before the run. He had concerns about the wind and I had a few concerns of my own. I'd never driven anything at speeds approaching 300 mph into standing water. I knew what it was like in my pickup on the freeway at 60. It would slip and slide once the tires began to hydroplane over the thin sheets of water trapped in the low spots on the highway's uneven surface.

That was scary enough.

This was something you had to mentally prepare for. The run could go flawlessly, but at some point you had to face the fact that you were going into unknown territory. How do you ask someone what to expect? The choice was mine. The crew had worked hard to get us where we were. I wasn't too happy with the situation, but I also knew Denis wouldn't let me do it if he really believed it wasn't doable. We decided to go for it. Some of the fastest recorded times set at Bonneville were done in the late fall, and some under wet conditions similar to what we were up against. What I didn't know was whether any of them were done on two wheels . . .

Once under way, it became immediately obvious that the prevailing winds, for whatever reason, had subsided. As a matter of fact, weatherwise, it was the calmest run I've yet to experience.

This was the pass we'd been waiting for. I pinned the throttle and for the first time, I could actually relax and enjoy the ride—it was that easy. The bike shifted through all four gears effortlessly. The wind remained calm and the tires gripped fairly well. I watched the tach and the speedometer as they both climbed steadily. As I approached the measured mile I noticed that we were in familiar territory.

Running through the trap under perfect conditions, one would think the record would be ours. We made it through all four gears. The engine never missed a beat, and there was no wind to be found. Top speed, 291 and some change. New day, same old shit.

Something let loose as we ripped through the measured mile. A loud bang startled me as a piece of something slammed against the composite body. As it turned out, it was a chain tensioner roller. Right about that time, the tranny also let go, adding to an already anxious moment.

And then there's the water.

The truth of the matter was, I got lucky. When the front tire first hit water, I thought I was going down. The front end pushed and the bike leaned awkwardly. As the rear tire joined the party, it slid in a similarly uncontrolled fashion. The thoughts going through my mind at this time were many. The biggest I suppose, was that this might hurt . . .

Oddly enough, as quickly as I lost control, it came back. Once the wheels realigned I was in complete control. I guess the transition from the rock-hard salt to the easily displaced salty liquid had its consequences. Once I was past the transition, everything was fine. Besides, the standing water only lasted for about a half-mile, and it didn't take long to get through it.

Back in the pits I explained to everyone that we had just made a perfect pass. The bike went as fast as it wanted to go, and 291 was all she had. Denis listened, but the eternal optimist had a difficult time believing.

After reviewing the run over and over from the trailer, and several more times at home on the laptop, we came to the conclusion that the only real chance *Tenacious II* had of breaking the record was a longer course with better traction and denser air. To our knowledge, only one such place existed that was at our disposal: Lake Gairdner, Australia.

It would be a slim chance at best, but in a bold attempt to make it to the top, it was decided that we would make a detour down under . . .

Chapter Seven
"All We Need is One G'Day"

It felt like one of the longest days of my life. For a person not comfortable flying, being forced to spend 24 hours hustling between crowded airports and having to sit in a flying *cattle car* for 14 hours didn't exactly top my list for the most exciting way to spend the day.

Add to that the fact that my best friend, Scott Jensen, and a supporting cast too long to mention, made sure I would be feeling my best for the long, bumpy haul. The all-night going away party consisted of copious amounts of alcohol, scantily clad

Tenacious II. This is where it began for me. To this day, this machine still holds the fastest one way pass on two wheels in Australia. *Photo courtesy of Larry Bliss*

women, and a number of unspeakable acts. The evening ended with a bizarre photo shoot taken by Mr. Jensen with a beautiful girl wearing nothing more than whipping cream, a hat, and a lovely smile. The pictures were a going away present that would someday cause me trouble.

Squeaky was no longer in the picture, but my new lady friend, who will remain nameless, was on assignment for Mr. Jensen, determined to make my last night at home a memorable one. All I could say was, "Job well done."

* * *

From the moment we landed, we knew it was going to be an interesting journey. There were about a dozen of us altogether, and each one greener than the next when it came to knowing the ways of Oz. We were immediately herded into a minivan limo with the steering wheel on the wrong side. The driver said "G'day," and put the pedal down. In no time we were weaving in an out of traffic on the wrong side of the road at a pace that was rather unnerving. Our driver swerved off the tarmac into an offbeat, motorhome rental yard.

Here we were, a dozen Yanks in the middle of a fairly large city, about to embark on a road trip of epic proportions in six of the funkiest diesel-powered motorhomes you'd ever laid eyes on. They, too, had the steering wheel on the wrong side, and a floor-mounted gearshift on the left. They did have a few creature comforts to offer, such as air conditioning and a gas-powered fridge. Neither of them worked.

After filling out the six-page questionnaire and signing the dotted line in blood, swearing we would never take their precious vehicles off the tarmac, we were free to go. We somehow failed to mention that we would be racing them across the outback for several hundred miles on rocky riverbeds and never-ending, silt-covered, dirt roads. Nor did we mention the fact that our final destination would be Lake Gairdner, one of the largest natural salt beds in the world.

In less than an Australian city block we were treated to a unique form of sign language from one of the locals. Apparently we had cut them off while trying to negotiate a lane change in our oversized, right-side-steering tour bus that we would fondly be calling home for the next two weeks. The gesture seemed friendly enough. Two fingers pointing in the air sort of like a backward peace sign. It was when the disenchanted driver yelled "Get stuffed!" that we realized the sign carried a different meaning in the Land of Oz. Our only saving grace was the fact that the next five tour buses of our group were having similar problems getting used to the ways of the road, and *each* managed to cut him off quite handily.

In keeping with the spirit of our great adventure, one of the younger crew members made an attempt at returning the gesture with an American greeting of the one-fingered variety. In spite of his shortcomings, the young lad had communicated with a local on a one-to-one basis. Our only hope was that our next encounter with the locals would be more civilized in nature.

We arrived at our hotel in the town of Adelaide, where we would be spending the next two days. This gave us a chance to recover from the jet lag associated with crossing several time zones, and also gave us some time to become acclimated to our new surroundings.

Port Augusta in South Australia would be the next rendezvous point. Denis had flown into Melbourne beforehand to pick up the race trailer and the bike. He had to buy a duallie to pull the trailer once he arrived, as the designated truck had somehow disappeared from the program. Racing overseas can become quite expensive at times . . .

With two days to kill before meeting up with Denis, we decided to use our time wisely . . . The men on the crew met in the lobby in hopes of being directed to the nearest watering hole.

From the registration desk you could see the bar. In that regard, our hotel was the perfect model of efficiency. Let it never be said that the Aussies don't have their priorities in order! The women also congregated in the lobby, organizing a quest of their own, hoping to take in some of the sights.

Once the women had left the building, we gathered around the barkeep and explained our situation. We told him (in the name of science), that we had decided to dedicate the rest of the afternoon to discovering the ultimate Australian brew. With his help, our two countries could become closer, sharing a common bond, sort of a goodwill expedition.

He agreed, for the sake of humanity and the hope of a very generous tip.

Pete Davis, a seasoned veteran in the art of brew tasting, had other ideas. He decided while we worked from the inside to bring our two countries closer together, it would be in all of our best interests if he were to voyage outside of our immediate surroundings for a wider viewpoint. It's unselfish acts like this that make our team so great. Pete would begin a journey steeped with tradition from days of old. A walkabout. Besides, rumor had it there was a beach not far from here where the Australian women ran around topless.

Bottles and cans in every shape and color emerged from behind the barkeep's counter one by one. In the end, it was narrowed down to three. VB (Victoria Bitter) was the most popular choice and most readily available brew in all of Australia. Its popularity rivaled that of Budweiser back home. Coopers, a locally brewed beer from Adelaide, was also quite popular. The problem was they made two different styles, red label or green. More testing had to be done . . .

In the end, it was unanimously decided that the beer of choice for the BUB Racing Team was Coopers in the red label. A rich, hearty flavor with alcohol content higher than that of a college freshman on spring break, our inebriated crew fondly referred to the wondrous nectar as "God's own piss."

Coopers was bottle fermented, which meant it formed a small layer of sediment at the base of the bottle. On occasion, as the hours waned during our intense testing session, the sediment was joined by pretzel pieces, sunflower seed shells, and the occasional cigarette butt. This tended to add a bitter taste to the local brew, the end result being quite similar to its larger counterpart, VB.

A semi-enclosed swimming pool was just beyond the bar, stocked with chairs and tables protected from the sun's intense rays. One by one the crew gathered, enjoying the cool breeze and shade. We discussed various topics: the extreme heat, the itinerary for the evening, the possibilities of Pete being arrested, etc.

Not long after, a wobbly figure appeared at the entrance to the pool. The shifting breeze revealed a scent of stale beer and sweat. The figure leaned forward and began an awkward jaunt toward pool's end. A scream of "Whoooeeeeee!!!" was heard as the fully clothed figure clumsily leapt from the concrete edge and splashed down in the midst of our congregation.

A half-hearted attempt at the "cannonball" position was recognized. He scored low for form and execution, though he did receive high marks for the enormous splash he created. As the wall of chlorinated water showered its intended targets, the assailant sank to the bottom of the pool like a lead sinker. Oddly enough, his wallet and all of its contents floated loosely to the top.

Our boy Pete had returned from his journey. Eventually he floated to the top and retrieved his belongings from the somewhat murky surface. In Native American slur, he recounted his travels. Apparently he had taken it upon himself to see to it that every bar from the hotel to the nudie beach had been explored. Being the thorough lad that he was, the ones he liked best he visited a second time on his trip back.

One bar in particular, the "Booze Brothers," was of particular interest to him. Their logo matched that of the logo on his T-shirt. Pete belongs to the Buell Brothers racing team back home. This extraordinary coincidence was something worth having a drink over. Truth be told, I think there were several.

He spoke of the beautiful beaches with brilliant white sand and half-naked women. It was obvious Mr. Davis liked it here. Out of respect for his day's achievements we bought him a Coopers and handed him a towel. After pointing him toward his room, we watched him saunter down the hallway. Like a steel ball in a pinball game, Pete bounced and rolled from one obstacle to the next, eventually making it to his room. His walkabout was finally over.

* * *

Dark smoke spewed from the exhaust pipes as the six diesel motorhomes were coaxed to life. One by one, the crew boarded their respective tour bus. After stopping for supplies at the local market, it was off to Port Augusta to meet up with Denis and the racer. We spent most of the day on the road, passing and being passed by the occasional land train and other various unique looking rigs.

A land train is a very large diesel truck, much larger than ours back home, that tows as many as four to five full-sized trailers at a time. Others only carried a single trailer, but the size of the trailer is massive. Long stretches of flat, boring, tarmac with little to look at except for the sporadic sightings of kangaroo road kill make this possible. The roads are exceptionally well maintained, possibly made easier by their lack of use.

We stayed the night in a hotel owned by an acquaintance of Denis. This would be the last civilized evening we would spend before heading out to the salt flats where we would set up shop for the next five days. It was here that we learned the ways of the bush and which deadly animals to steer clear of.

Australia is home to some of the most deadly creatures on the planet, snakes that will stop your heart and kill you in minutes, and spiders that will drop a full-grown man and add his name to the obituary column the following morning.

And then there are the kangaroos. We were told these lovable, fuzzy creatures were equally deadly under the right circumstances. Their means of defense is their long claws. They've been known to rear back against their powerful tail and frantically claw apart their predators—including the unsuspecting tourist.

The best advice? Walk loud, we were told. As long as the creatures weren't startled, they would usually go away rather than go into defense mode. The mandatory middle-of-the-night urination ritual had to be redefined. Whenever any of us left the motorhome to give back some of Adelaide's finest, we would slam the door, stomp on the ground, and keep our eyes wide open. Returning Coopers to its native soil could at times be risky.

Early the next morning we loaded up and pointed ourselves in the direction of Lake Gairdner. It would take several hours to get there, with the last hundred miles or so on a road that wasn't paved.

Being the racers that we were, the dirt road became somewhat of a challenge. The dry, silty surface gave us the opportunity to practice broad-sliding our rigs. I can honestly say that, up until then, I had no idea what it felt like to pitch an overloaded motorhome into a corner at over 100 kilometers per hour. I know it now!

Every time my traveling companion, Howard Carte, would start to dose off, I'd speed it up a little. Driving hard into a slippery corner, the front wheels would push, the top-heavy beast would lean, and many of our belongings would fall from the cupboards and crash to the floor. The important thing was we were keeping entertained. It was a long, dirty drive.

As long as you kept your foot in it, it would eventually come around. Getting sideways in one of these oversized beasts had its moments. On more than one occasion the front end pushed so bad we ended up sliding off the road, careening off annoying obstacles such as large rocks or nasty ditches. Bouncing off the ceiling of our makeshift racer, Howard soon found himself wide awake. Mission accomplished . . .

At one point we decided to stop and see how everything was holding up. The six white motorhomes had all acquired a dusty brown tint. The race trailer was also not as bright and shiny as it once was. When we opened it up, the streamliner was completely covered with a heavy layer of brown silt. The toolboxes and their contents, along with all the cupboards and chests, had the same brown tinge. When we finally reached the salt, we would have our work cut out for us.

A few hours later we were finally there. My first thought as we crested the final hill and looked down over the great expanse of white, was that of anticipation. I could already see myself barreling across the salt with reckless abandon. I could picture the vibrating view from the cockpit, the feeling of being strapped in so tight I could barely move. The taste of salt as the sweat ran down my face inside my fire-retardant liner that was crushed beneath my helmet. All this and more. This is what we came for. We were finally here . . .

* * *

Our weathered caravan slowly approached the apron of Lake Gairdner. The endless miles of dirty, dusty, unpaved transit were behind us. As our wheels touched down onto the rock-hard surface, the annoying vibrations stopped. The squeaking and creaking noises of the abused tour buses went silent as the dirty tires rolled effortlessly across the user-friendly surface.

It was an eerie feeling making our entrance onto the salt bed. All eyes were upon us. It's not everyday that a group of Yanks make the long journey across continents to compare toys with people from another land. But here we were. We pulled into the makeshift pits and stepped out onto the pristine surface. At this very moment there was no other place on God's green earth we would rather be . . .

Denis met up with the "who's who" of the event while the crew went about the arduous task of cleaning up the racer and all of the contents of the trailer. The motorhomes had to be left behind, about 500 yards back in the racers' camping area. Only tow vehicles, race trailers, and pit supplies were allowed on the salt. A pressurized washer was set up at the base of the hill and all vehicles leaving the salt had to stop and be hosed down. No salt was to leave the lakebed. They had their own set of rules, and we were happy to oblige.

Everyone had a job to do, and it was my job to familiarize myself with the course. I hitched a ride with one of the locals and took a quick spin up and down the course. They were running a little behind schedule. Another American team led by Chuck Salman had made the trip across the pond and had taken it upon themselves to prepare the surface. Salman had one of his crewmembers pulling a drag across the salt. The course markers were still being put up and the timing lights were yet to be seen.

Back home everything was ready before I showed up. Denis would always see to that. We were serious about what we were doing, and the costs involved made it very important that our time was used wisely.

The Aussies were also very serious about racing. They just went about things at a different pace. They were much more laid back than us Americans. They had a favorite saying, "No worries, mate," which meant exactly that. It would get done when it got done. There was no need to worry about it. I was having a tough time learning their laid-back ways. I wanted to go racing, and their inability to stay on schedule only added to my anxiety.

I had a lot to learn about the "down under" ways. Over time, I grew to appreciate their methods. They were a less stressful bunch than our uptight, life-in-the-fast-lane boys and girls back home. They knew how to enjoy life. They put less pressure on themselves, and it showed in their happy-go-lucky demeanor. But dammit, I wanted to go racing, and they were holding up the show!

When I returned to the pits everything was clean. The bike looked like it did when we originally loaded it in the trailer back home. The canopy was up and our pit was in order. We were all dressed up with nowhere to go.

Denis had heard that they were having trouble with the timing lights and that it would be another day before anyone could run. I was pissed, but somehow also relieved. It gave us more time to go over the bike and our own game plan. Besides, we had a new part on the bike, a high-output ignition coil we were trying that was giving us some problems. Hopefully this would allow us to work through it.

The racer still had to make it through tech inspection, which it would pass with flying colors. All bragging aside, it was the most sophisticated piece of equipment of the entire meet. Next came the safety inspection. The bike was examined from head to toe. Safety is always a serious matter in speed racing. Back home, an ambulance was always on hand in case of an emergency. The nearest town was only 20 minutes away, and in the event of a life threatening injury, Salt Lake City was just over 100 miles away, 30 minutes by helicopter.

Here, things were quite different. The nearest town was over 200 miles away, and there was no ambulance to be found. They had a "flying doctor" on call, but even he would take a while to arrive if needed.

Instead, the Kimba Fire Brigade was at our service. These young, athletic, adventurous race fans would be responsible for keeping us alive in the event of an emergency. Typical Australian logic: no worries. Don't get me wrong. I'm sure they were properly trained in administering CPR, and their youthful courage (the oldest of the bunch couldn't have been over 30) may have come in useful had they been required to pull an unconscious victim from his burning wreckage, but it made me wonder how good my chances really were should I have to depend on these young lads to keep me alive for several hours until a trained professional could finally examine my broken, bleeding body.

The good news was they were a lot of fun.

These boys knew a good time when they saw one. What better assignment than to be sent to the outback for a week to watch some of the fastest motorized vehicles on the planet sail across a salt lake at nearly half the speed of sound. Not to mention, it was a great place to party . . .

Back home we have *Good Morning America,* a popular news show that starts the day for millions of Americans. Down under, they have *Good Morning Australia.* Motorsports are such a big thing in their country that they decided to broadcast their show live for the entire week on the salt. Having a serious racing effort from the United States competing against them in this type of venue was news, which they were happy to exploit on a daily basis. In fact, for the entire meet, the morning show was filmed from our pit.

For five days straight, Australia awoke to the likes of Denis and myself recapping the previous day's events. They tracked our progress, put up with some of Denis's bad jokes, and watched with great interest how the boys from across the pond fared against their own. Luckily for us, when it was all said and done, we had the fastest time of the meet. Not only were we the fastest ever on two wheels in their country, we also went faster than any of their streamlined cars. They threw everything they had at us all week. The bottom line was, on this trip, we were the cream of the crop . . .

* * *

We didn't have an easy time of it. From day one we had problems. A new high-output coil was being used in hopes of gaining a little more power. It never worked properly and would make the bike miss at high rpm. We had the original coil with us for backup, but it would be a major project to replace. After several unsuccessful runs, it was finally decided to go back to square one. The crew worked most of the night removing the faulty coil and wiring, and installed the original unit. I was a bit discouraged, knowing we were giving away a few extra ponies. We came to kick ass and take names. Now we were just trying to survive.

There were numerous other problems and a few close calls. On one occasion I nearly took out the entire Kimba Fire Brigade. I was running midcourse when a huge gust of wind hit me from the right side. Before I knew it, I was blown off line and heading right for them! My speedometer reading was over 260 mph when I was blown in their direction.

I have to mention that the boys weren't running on all eight cylinders at the time. The previous night was spent in celebration. The crew had thrown a party in celebration of my birthday. The Kimba Fire Brigade showed up in full force, offering to help with the inebriation process.

We were busy having margarita wars when they showed up to lend a hand. This was something new to them, and as it turned out, very entertaining for us. We had brought along two of our "race version" margarita machines. The blenders had two-stroke engines, one on race fuel, the other sporting just a taste of methanol for added performance. It must also be noted that Howard's (my weary traveling companion) was sporting a custom-made straight pipe that made you wince with pain when running at full throttle.

It's the simple things that make life so rewarding. Such as watching innocent young men from the opposite side of our planet, tasting a favorite drink from back home for the first time. Watching them guzzle down the frosty contents and seeing a salty mustache form on their upper lip.

Watching them reel with pain as brain freeze sets in.

Sharing a laugh with the *Good Morning Australia* crew who, only moments before, were also reeling with the same pain but were much happier now that they were not alone. These were great times. Memories I'll always treasure.

One of the younger members of the brigade was so bent on being just like us that I had to seize the moment. On the table next to one of the two-stroke blenders was a large bottle of tequila. It had to be around a half-gallon in size. There was still well over an inch and a half of the harsh liquid remaining in the bottom. He held up the bottle into the light and asked the inevitable. It was almost like he was challenging our drinking capabilities.

I responded as any red-blooded American would whose main objective was to see his naïve counterpart suffer.

I lied . . .

"Back home, that much is no big deal." I was laying it on pretty thick, "We'd just down it, mate . . . my sister could drink that much."

"Serious?" He stared closer at the contents in the bottle, determined to be one of us. He looked to his friends for encouragement. They were just as eager to witness the feat, and were also just as willing to lie for the sake of entertainment.

"Well then, no worries," he said, as he tilted the large bottle toward the sky.

That was a lot of tequila. We watched as the determined young lad gulped and swallowed. His eyes watered, closed, crossed, and possibly even bled . . . but he kept drinking. The party fell strangely silent as all eyes watched his self-induced sacrifice. He kept the bottle tilted until the final drop was emptied. When he finally lowered his arm, in his mind he was one of us.

He wearily examined the large bottle. He was proud. Soon he would be nauseous. "Damn, mate. That much?" he was amazed at what studs us Americans must surely be.

"Well . . . maybe not *that* much!" I finally let in. The whole place burst into laughter. His teammates toasted him and took turns taking a pull from the alcohol of choice, but none dared equal his performance. He was the man of the moment, a hero to his peers. Not long after, he was seen practicing the art of projectile vomiting behind one of our motorhomes.

Another to get caught with their guard down was the anchor lady herself. A trained professional who made her living in the public's eye seemed like the perfect candidate. She was attractive, smart, and apparently had a newfound love for our frothy beverage. Howard slipped a rubber cockroach into her glass when she wasn't looking, then topped it off for good measure. As she worked her way toward the bottom, the disgusting bug revealed itself to the "always composed" morning show host.

"You bastard!" she squealed, as Howard came to her rescue and pulled the bug from her glass with his bare hands. He then tilted his head back and dropped the marinated mascot into his mouth and began to chew. All eyes watched as the rubber insect was manhandled and chewed to a salty death by a brave soul who acted unselfishly to restore the morning show host's honor. American bravery at its finest . . .

As mentioned earlier, at over 260 mph, I was blown off course and heading straight for the Kimba Fire Brigade. I missed them by probably 50 feet, but at those speeds and being at the mercy of the wind, it seemed much closer than that. When I returned to the pits, we watched the run on the computer so Denis and the crew could see what I was up against. When the wind hit, my handlebars went nearly full lock, trying to compensate to no avail. Future runs would have to be postponed until the winds subsided.

On another pass, at high speed, the front end wobbled terribly. As I approached nearly 280 mph, the front end shook so violently that I had to abort the run. The vibration was so bad that I couldn't see where I was going. It was also very difficult to maintain control since steering input was severely sacrificed due to the nature of the problem. When I finally brought the ill-handling machine to a stop, I was shaking a little myself.

I asked Denis to have a look at the front tire. I already had a pretty good idea what the problem was. We had recently installed aluminum discs on either side of the front wheel to help reduce aerodynamic drag. I never liked the discs because it made it very difficult to check air pressure. Because of this, I was pretty sure the procedure was occasionally neglected.

As suspected, the front tire had lost air pressure during the pass. We usually run about 80 psi (pounds per square inch) in the front tire. We found there was less than 30 psi in the tire when we returned. I was a little disappointed that I was put in harm's way simply because a procedure had been overlooked, and I expressed my concerns to Denis and the crew. In his defense, he said the air pressure had been checked before the run, but that the valve stem cap wasn't in place when the tire was inspected upon my return. Whatever the case, it scared the hell out of me, and I was promised this would never happen again . . .

And then there was the final day on the salt. Our last chance.

We had come to be champions. The fastest. Anything else wouldn't do. On the final day, we still hadn't reached our goal. Once again, the wind picked up and we were forced to wait. Wayne O'Grady, the man in charge of the meet, kept us up to date on wind conditions across the course. Everyone else was pretty much through. Blown engines, deteriorating tires, and even a few Aussie records were already in the books. Most of the participants were now more concerned about finding adequate shade and a cold brew than making another pass.

Tension was high among our crew. The bike was wounded. We had a vibration in the engine that was an inevitable death sentence. The question wasn't if, but when. We came too far to just quit. The decision was made that we would keep running until either the record was ours, or until *Tenacious II* gave up the ghost.

Waiting was hard for me. One good pass could change everything. Everyone worked so hard to get us to where we were, but we were running on reserve. The event organizers were ready to close up shop. The wind refused to go away. Our crew was beat up and tired. And, we had a motor that was pretty well used up.

We lined up at the end of the course and readied ourselves for war. We were not going down without a fight.

It seemed like hours, but finally the wind decided to take a break. I suited up and climbed inside. John strapped me in and wished me well. Denis gave me his best and told me not to hold anything back. The starter motor was engaged to the crank and readied for deployment.

Suddenly, Wayne O'Grady came up and put a stop to the whole operation. "It seems we've got company," he warned. "There's a kangaroo on the track!"

Only in Australia . . .

I couldn't believe it. We finally had our chance and now we had to wait again. Our window of opportunity was slowly beginning to close. If the wind picked back up, it might already be over.

"No worries, we'll run the little bugger off," Wayne assured.

Imagine making that final pass at over 300 mph. All eyes are upon you. *Good Morning Australia's* camera crew has you in their sights. Everyone in the pits is standing on their tiptoes straining to see. The organization that invited us across the pond is finally getting their money's worth. It's that very moment that dreams are made of. And then at midcourse, this bouncing marsupial finds its way into your path. WHAM! Kangaroo burgers for 20.

The thoughts bouncing through my head were many. It's a little unnerving to think of all the possibilities . . . so many things
that can go wrong. My dad has a saying that has always stuck with
me. "If there's a bullet out there with your name on it, it's going to
find you. It's the one that says 'To whom it may concern,' that you
need to watch out for."

As was earlier feared, the winds returned. I climbed from the
cockpit and sat in wait. It's hard to keep the adrenaline flowing at
times like this. You get amped up, and then let back down. This
process happens over and over. It drains you both physically and
mentally. We feared that Wayne and his organization might finally pull the plug. It didn't happen. No worries, remember . . .

And then the moment finally came.

The salt flats grew quiet and Wayne appeared with a look of relief
about his windburned face. He spoke with Denis and John, and then
with myself. "The winds have settled, but we're running out of time.
If this isn't a record pass, we're going to have to close up shop. My
mates need time to tear down the course and tidy up the place."

We'd been out on the salt since 5:30 in the morning. We'd
been out here at that time each day for five days straight. It was
now a little after 10 and it was painfully obvious that even the kangaroos were growing impatient.

It was now or never.

I reentered *Tenacious II* for the final time. There weren't a lot of
words spoken as I was strapped in for one last go. Everything had
already been said. I received the thumbs up from John and began my
final descent down the salt from behind the tow vehicle. Everything
had to be perfect in order for us to accomplish our mission.

The tow vehicle was a bit gutless and took more than the usual
amount of time to get us up to speed. With that in mind, we
backed up almost a quarter-mile in front of the usual starting position. This allowed us to not waste any valuable real estate while

trying to build up speed before the measured mile at midcourse.

I followed the tow vehicle for about a half-mile before releasing. Even then, we hadn't reached optimum release speed, but I was determined to pick up the pace early. The winds weren't completely gone, but at least they were tolerable. As the motor picked up rpm, the unwelcome vibration returned. I made the shift from first to second at around 170 mph. The shift was clean. So far, so good.

Second gear is always amazing. Acceleration in second gear is so powerful that you have to be careful not to light up the tire and lose momentum from unnecessary wheelspin. Too much wheelspin can literally tear the tire apart. Chunks of rubber can actually rip from the tire's carcass and throw the wheel out of balance, or worse yet, cause the tire to blow out or lose air.

This would not be one of those times. I was spot-on. Wheel spin was minimal and acceleration was maximized. Even with the engine's damaging vibration, the motor felt powerful and loose. The rpm climbed at an unusually high pace. As mentioned earlier, the best way I can describe the sensation of second gear in *Tenacious II* is the feeling you get from takeoff in a jet airliner barreling down the runway. You're pushed back deep in your seat as the g-forces take over. It's quite a rush.

Second gear takes me to nearly 250, and at a record pace. I shift to third and once again, the shift is clean. They say that sometimes an engine runs its best right before it lets go, and ours was running stronger and faster than ever before. The vibration was still there, but it definitely wasn't holding us back. Here I was, doing damn near 270 mph, and I was just barely past the 2-mile marker. This was the run we were waiting for!

Everyone held their breath as I reached for the final gear. So many times the transmission would fail and the run would have to be aborted. We were having the run of our life, and it was possible that if only we could have one more clean shift, we would go home heroes. I'm sure no one was more nervous than John. The transmission was his baby. Everyone wanted nothing more than to give John the elusive "attaboy," if only we could make the shift just once more.

"Click."

That's all it took. A press of a button and we were in fourth gear and moments away from climbing into the record books. If John were a little better looking I could've given him a big kiss for a job well done. As it was, the "attaboy," was recorded and we were on our way.

275, 280, 285. By the 3-mile marker I'm pretty much convinced we've done it. We've got tons of room to continue accelerating, and at the current pace, the record's ours.

That's when all hell breaks loose.

Somewhere between the 3- and 4-mile markers what we feared most finally happens. One of the connecting rods breaks and punches a hole through the block and starts the self-destruction process inside *Medusa*. Oil spews everywhere and smoke fills the engine compartment.

The impact from the rod smashing through the engine block hammers the bike with a sudden, unexpected jolt. I fight to regain control as the bike wobbles dangerously close to the ragged edge. The handlebars instantly go lock-to-lock as I counter the jolt, which is followed by an unexpected weight transfer as the 20-foot streamliner goes from acceleration mode to deceleration in the blink of an eye.

Once I have the bike straightened out and have regained my composure (sort of), I find myself coasting through the measured mile. Oddly enough, even though there are only three pistons and connecting rods left, the motor is still running. I reach up and switch off the ignition, hoping to salvage whatever is left of the now deceased engine.

My problems are far from over. The bike is now coasting down from nearly 300 mph, and there is a good chance it will be on fire before I can get her stopped. Even with the proven capabilities of our parachutes, it still takes a great deal of time to get the bike completely stopped at those speeds.

As the bike slows, smoke begins to fill the cockpit with me. By the time I'm ready to deploy the skids, I can barely see. It's a little scary not knowing whether it's safe to breathe in the smoke-filled air, but you really have no choice. I put down the skids and bring the wounded racer to rest on the right skid. While trying to take in only baby breaths through my nose, I release a heavy sigh, knowing that at least the fear of crashing is behind me.

As the smoke becomes thicker and denser, I scramble to release my harness and reach for the latch to open the cockpit. I remember hoping that help is nearby, fearing that if there were a fire on board, the rush of fresh air into the cockpit might make for an unwanted conclusion. I pop the release and push the canopy open. Fresh air fills my lungs and dissipates the dark cloud of smoke.

Much to my relief, there is no fire. When the rod punched through the engine block, oil spewed in every direction, coating *Medusa* and the entire engine compartment. The heavy smoke was the result of hot oil making contact with the expired powerplant, which pooled at the bottom of the engine compartment before finding its way out onto the salt. A dark puddle formed underneath with a few large chunks of aluminum from the engine block and various rod and piston fragments thrown into the mix for added color and texture.

The Kimba Fire Brigade was the first to show up, followed closely by my crew and just about everyone else involved with the event. Denis was at the far end of the course and took longer to reach us than the rest. From his vantage point things weren't yet clear. Was he approaching a crash site? Did another bloody kangaroo get in the way? Just what the hell happened?

"It looks like you've got a leg out of bed, mate." One of the course workers explained. That was his version of the rod breaking through the cases. We couldn't help but laugh. The Aussies find humor in everything, even at the most peculiar moments.

The bike was examined, the puddle of oil removed, and the run relived in painstaking detail as the crippled machine was prepared to go back in the race trailer for the final ride back to the pits.

Just then, Wayne O'Grady showed up with some interesting information. He'd just received word from the timekeepers that even with a blown engine we managed to coast through the lights at 289 mph. That was good enough for top time of the meet. Not only were we the fastest motorcycle to ever set foot on Australian soil, but even the high-powered streamlined cars couldn't contend with the pace we had set.

John and Denis started crunching the numbers, and it was concluded that before the engine let go, we had gone in excess of 297 mph and had done so in just over 3 miles. We were on a record pace when *Tenacious II* let go. We were oh so close . . .

Part Two
The Birth of Big Red

Chapter Eight
A New Era

Back home we had a lot of work to do. By all accounts, the record should have been ours. Australia was our big chance, and we failed to take advantage of it. The bike was good, but was it really *that* good? We studied the data and also did a little soul searching.

There were a few areas that definitely could be improved upon. One was the weight. With me in it, the overall weight was around 2,000 pounds. The other was the aerodynamics. *Tenacious II* had a coefficient of drag that measured around 0.2. It was good, but at

After retiring Tenacious II, this would be my new office for the next couple of seasons. *Photo courtesy of Larry Bliss*

high speed, we found it wasn't *that* good. A more streamlined shape would be a definite bonus.

The problem was how to achieve this. The machine weighed what it weighed. It was already built. You couldn't just send the streamliner to Jenny Craig. And to give it a new shape, just how could that be done?

There was really only one true answer: Build a new machine.

Denis has built many streamliners over the years. It is his passion. He'll tell you getting the record back is all that matters, but I've never been quite convinced of that. It's like anything else. It's all about the *journey.* A major part of the journey is building the bike itself. In all the years that I've known him, he's *always* been building a streamliner. Some people collect baseball cards. Denis builds streamliners. It's his addiction.

And so the decision was made that a new streamliner would be constructed. There would be major changes in the design. Less weight. Less drag.

Better brakes . . .

A clean sheet of paper offered lots of advantages. Things that didn't work before could simply be eliminated. Things we liked, we could improve upon. For example, it was decided that instead of using the traditional tubular steel frame enclosed in fiberglass, the new design would be made almost exclusively from composite materials. The tubular chassis was tossed, and a carbon fiber and Kevlar monocoque design would be utilized in its place. This meant that the outer composite "shell" was actually pulling double-duty as the chassis also.

We were borrowing aerospace technology which had already become the norm in Formula One auto racing. Eliminating the internal structure and replacing it with a modern day exoskeleton saved us 500-plus pounds of unnecessary weight. The other benefit was we were no longer stuck with our original shape.

The old shape was pretty efficient up to around 270 mph. After that, it lost stability. One thought was that the air was packing against the upright windshield and causing severe turbulence and drag. Whatever the case, the old design was shelved and a newly refined, more aerodynamic shape would take its place.

Safety is always a big issue in land speed racing, and we had some areas that could be improved upon. One of the biggest was the steering mechanism. *Tenacious II* had a pivoting canopy. When it was opened, the handlebars lifted up with it. The dangerous part about it was that my hands were wrapped around the bars. If it flew open in a crash, my hands and arms would also come out and become quite vulnerable. In later runs I was able to convince Denis and John to add an internal strap to help keep the lid on tight.

In the new bike, there are no handlebars at all. Instead, two joysticks are used for the steering duties. Each attaches to a pivoting arm, which either pushes or pulls a cable attached directly to the triple clamp. I used a similar design in one of my first gravity-powered go karts when I was a kid. *Simple is good.*

The joysticks straddle my torso with the handles tucked in neatly at my sides. To turn the wheel to the right, I pull on the right stick and push with the left. To turn the wheel to the left, the opposite is true. Just remember that this is just to *turn* the wheel. To actually steer left while in *motion,* I would pull on the right stick to initiate lean angle, then follow it up as the bike slowly changed direction.

The hand controls themselves are pretty slick. Remember Tom Cruise in *Top Gun?* The black control-grip he was squeezing and maneuvering his fighter jet with is virtually the same as what I have in my cockpit—only I have two of them. I have the same red trigger, the same switches and buttons strategically placed for deployment at a moments notice. The same four-way toggle switch at the top with multifunction capabilities. The same problem always trying to avoid teenage screaming groupies hounding me for autographs wherever I go.

Well–three out of four ain't bad . . .

* * *

For me, waiting was always the hard part. The first streamliner I drove *(Tenacious II)* took eight years to build. It was a little easier that time around because I didn't know what I was getting myself into and was in no hurry to get myself killed. But as expected, I survived. And now I've got the bug to go back. The new bike will take much less time to build, but even three years compared to eight is still a long time. I'm very grateful to my crew for all their hard work, but sometimes it's just downright hard to wait patiently in the wings while Father Time marches on.

I remember when a cluster of tanks had to be designed and fabricated, Denis and I had very different opinions on what was important. The oil, fuel, and water tanks when completed resembled a Rubik's Cube. They were interlocked and compressed into a neat and tidy, compact unit. Made from carbon fiber and Kevlar materials, the finished product was really a work of art. My complaint was, I didn't think the two months that it took Denis to make the darn things was really necessary. Stainless-steel or even aluminum tanks would have been sufficient and could have been built in a week.

There was a chance of us testing a full season sooner had similar decisions been made. Ultimately, it is sometimes good that you don't always get what you ask for. As it stands, the tanks are the most beautiful I've ever seen, and if equal care and attention is given to more critical components *which very possibly might save my ass someday,* who am I to complain?

Racing season for an LSR machine is ridiculously short. If your budget limits you to staying within the continental United States, Bonneville is your only real option. One of our concerns once the new bike was complete was the time needed to test before actually making any land-speed record attempts. Normally, Bonneville isn't dry and hard until mid- to late summer. If we waited until then to begin our testing, we would lose a whole year just gearing up for an all-out record attempt. With that in mind, we are always looking for a new lakebed to explore that we could possibly test on before the actual racing season began.

In early September of 2002, Denis, myself, and a fellow employee of our company who goes by the name "Buzzy" set out on an unexpected journey. The plan was to go to Phoenix, Arizona, to look at a couple of welding robots that were purchased from the now-bankrupt Excelsior Henderson Company. This was the first time Buzzy had been on a road trip with us, and in his defense, none of us knew what was in store on the ride back home.

If you look on a Nevada road map at the mysterious and often controversial Area 51, you will see a dry lakebed named Mud Lake. A border separating Area 51 from civilian life runs smack-dab down the center of the lakebed. In actuality, as we would soon find out, the border is just a wooden fence with suspended wire keeping trespassers at bay.

Since we were in the vicinity, Denis asked if we wouldn't mind taking a detour to look at a possible testing ground for the racer.

"It's probably only 20 minutes or so out of the way." When he's in this mode, there's really no denying him. "Look, right here," he continued, pointing at the map. He had this big, shit-eatin' grin.

"Mud Lake. Says so right here." His eyes were alive with excitement. He was like a kid who was just granted entry into Disneyland because he "happened to be in the vicinity."

So like three lost souls in search of the Holy Grail, off we went into the vast Nevada desert searching for a new place to try our toy. Once you get near Area 51, an eerie feeling comes over you. You know . . . like you're not *supposed* to be there. Anyway, the stories start coming, each of us spinning a bigger yarn than the last. We come upon a couple of giant, vacated hangars. At one time these housed something rather large . . . something significant.

Something they wanted kept far away.

We pull up to the second hangar after seeing a car and a pickup parked outside, life forms that might be able to point us in the right direction. An older gentleman wearing blue jeans and a button-up blue shirt walked out to greet us, or maybe just to see what the hell we were doing on his property. We admitted to being somewhat confused on how to find the lakebed, so he gave Denis directions and sent us on our way. I remember Buzzy telling Denis and me that the old coot was probably an alien . . . or something worse. He joked that if we ever came back, the old man would probably have mysteriously changed sexes, and the next time we saw him he would be a woman. Strange thoughts run through that man's head . . .

So for the next half hour or so, we drive around lost and disappointed. Keep in mind we are already past our 20-minute projected time frame, and we haven't even left the old man's property. Going against God and nature, and everything that's right, we double back and do the unthinkable. Three grown men in a dual-lie pickup no less. More testosterone than a bull on Viagra during mating season. We pull up in front of the hangar, and Denis (with his head held low), goes back inside to ask directions once again. The Cardinal Sin of manliness.

I'll be damned if the old man in the worn blue jeans and a button-up blue shirt didn't come to the big front hangar door with long blonde hair and breasts—Buzzy was right! We looked her (him?) over from head to toe in disbelief. Area 51 . . . what a strange place. It was only later that we found out this was the old man's wife. Denis had pulled a fast one and sent her to the door in his place. It was a mere coincidence that the two were dressed alike.

Back we went, bouncing and careening off the cruel desert floor. We found the rock-cluttered dirt road in question and proceeded down the path to righteousness and lakebeds. Luckily for us, this little excursion was only "20 minutes out of the way." Another 30 minutes passed, and we had yet to reach our destination. We had to cross several riverbeds and washes, not to mention treading ever-so-lightly over sun-baked, sharp pointy rocks.

We stopped to take a better look through the binoculars. I jumped in the back of the truck and scanned the hazy distance. There was a reflection of sunlight bouncing off a faraway windshield. We were not alone. We waited patiently, but the vehicle never moved. Through the high-powered lens I could see the lakebed . . . and the fence. We piled back in and pointed the duallie toward the "promised land." Ten minutes later we finally reached paydirt.

The surface was flat, but the texture was rough and uneven. We drove a ways trying to get a feel for what it might be like in the racer. It had good spots and bad. It also had that damned fence. We could no longer see the reflective glare off the windshield of the vehicle we assumed was watching us. It had somehow disappeared. We decided to have a closer look at the fence that kept civilian life and military secrets separate. Sure enough, there were sensors lining the boundaries a few feet behind the fence, spread approximately an eighth-mile apart.

The lakebed didn't meet our standards so we were forced to leave. Before we did, as is the way of the wild, we found it necessary to mark our territory. For reasons only known to him, Denis found it necessary to leave his mark on the military side—pushing the envelope, so to speak.

Rather than return the way we came in, Denis was sure he knew a shortcut we could take that would probably be much smoother and shorter. We would instead continue on, driving around the base of the lakebed onto what appeared to be a dirt road (or wagon trail) that looked like it hadn't been traveled since the invention of rubber tires.

At the base of the lakebed we crossed the sacred line. Buzzy gave a look of concern, but Denis just smiled. "Don't worry, it's a shortcut. We'll just follow this dirt road and be out of here in no time." If we only knew what we were getting ourselves into . . .

I'm here to tell you, this road (and I'm using the term "road" very loosely) had not seen use in years. It was more of a rock path than anything else. Only a couple of miles into it we realized there was no turning back. The steep, sandy hills and continuous washes we somehow navigated downhill would be impossible to pass in the other direction. The sun was straight up and everything with half a brain had taken cover until nightfall.

Except for us.

We limped along, stopping occasionally to move the bigger rocks off the "road" so we could continue in a generally forward direction. On more than one occasion we were sure the tires would burst by the ragged terrain we were forced to drive through. Buzzy opened the ice chest Denis had brought along and pulled an odd looking bottle from the lukewarm water. It was a large, Miller beer bottle filled with water. The label read something to the effect of "Miller Disaster Relief Water." It was an omen staring him in the face.

It was given to Denis by a friend after a tornado tore through his hometown of Siren, Wisconsin. *Maybe the bottle was cursed . . . * You could almost feel the buzzards circling overhead as we bravely pushed forward. Off in the distance a paved road slowly came into view. We were saved! *Or so we thought . . .*

The wagon trail and pavement refused to meet. Ours ran parallel to the road, but never got closer than a couple of miles. And then it started to turn in the wrong direction! "We'll all laugh about this later, boys," Denis chuckled. It was a tough room, and laughter was hard to come by. Buzzy stared longingly out the window as the paved road disappeared from sight.

Eventually the two paths crossed and we once again made it back to civilization. Our "20-minute" detour actually put us about four hours behind schedule. I can't help but wonder if as we wandered around lost somewhere in Area 51, someone was watching us.

* * *

In October of 2002, Denis went back to Bonneville to take in Speed Week. He wanted to be there when the late Don Vesco attempted to go 500 mph in his four-wheel-driven, turbine-powered car. The motor he was using was out of a military chopper. *Mucho power!* Unfortunately, Vesco had serious mechanical problems and was forced to sit this one out.

Another hero of the salt flats, Nolan White, was the class of the field. A few weeks earlier, Nolan had set the record for piston-powered streamlined cars at 413 mph. He was back and ready to up the ante. For an official record you have to make two passes, one in each direction. His plan was to run the course from the opposite direction first, then turn around and make his second pass (which he intended to be the faster of the two), heading toward safer ground and hopefully into the record books. (When the course is run in the opposite direction, there is less runoff with the ultimate stopping point being the highway.)

Disaster struck for Nolan at the end of a near picture-perfect run averaging 422 mph through the fourth mile trap . . . his top speed was even greater. Knowing the danger of running in this direction at Bonneville, Nolan had planned on only accelerating through the fourth of five timed mile traps, intentionally leaving extra room to decelerate.

When he deployed the first parachute, it tore free of the machine, failing to scrub off speed. The second and third chutes were also deployed, and one by one they too had failed. A similar incident happened to Nolan in an earlier run in August, but he managed to steer safely off course into a remote area where the heavy slurry of salt and mud brought him to a stop. On this occasion he had only two parachutes. A third was later added, but proved meaningless in the end.

His only option was to exit the racecourse in search of open ground. In his attempt to do this, the car slid sideways, dug in and flipped several times. One of two engines was thrown 300 feet from the vehicle. It was estimated that Nolan was still traveling in the neighborhood of 300 mph when he lost control and crashed. Nolan died three days later of massive head trauma. Other injuries sustained in the crash included broken ribs and a punctured lung.

The reason I share this information is the fact that our new bike was designed with maximum efficiency in mind. The tail area is so narrow that there isn't enough room to run a backup parachute. From the moment I was made aware of this, I had my concerns. Brakes on streamliners are pretty much useless above 150 mph. Parachutes work great at speed . . . but sometimes they fail. On our first machine, we encountered only two parachute failures, one on the high-speed chute (a tiny, 18-inch diameter ribbon chute) and, more importantly, one on the main chute.

When our main parachute failed, what had happened was the pilot chute opened and drew the main chute from the canister, and somehow it made contact with the pilot chute and inverted (turned inside out, wrapping itself around the pilot chute). I was traveling well over 280 mph when this happened. Luckily I had a backup parachute, which I quickly deployed. *No worries,* as they say. The only casualty from this incident was a heavily soiled Fruit of the Loom.

I have to make it abundantly clear that our crew is 100 percent behind me as far as safety is concerned. Denis and John have taken great pains to ensure my safety in the new machine. After the incident with Nolan White, I expressed my concerns. Denis called a meeting with the entire crew. I wanted them to take another look at what could be done to install a backup parachute.

The meeting was pretty slick, actually. I felt bad because they already had so much work ahead of them just in building the darn thing. What I was asking would mean even more work, not to mention the added time and money also required to complete the task.

John was the first to voice his opinion and made no qualms about letting me know that this was not Nolan White's streamliner, and they were not part of Mr. White's crew. His point was they were doing everything to the best of their abilities. No shortcuts were being taken. Nolan White's streamliner may have been one of the fastest of its day, but it was a little cruder in fabrication and design than what we were building. If there was a safety issue that needed to be addressed, it would be. And it would be done right—period.

He also reminded me that once we had the record behind us, he was going to take a turn behind the wheel as a sort of victory lap. He wasn't about to build anything that he might be injured in. All the time his voice was firm and direct. I thought maybe I had pissed him off. To the contrary, he was being sincere. He wanted me to know that they would do whatever it took to make it right. That was good enough for me.

What they came up with was nothing shy of brilliant. There was only room for two canisters at the rear of the bike. One for the high-speed chute, and one for the main chute. In order for us to have a third chute we needed either more room for another canister, or a new way of thinking. The latter was chosen.

Enter NASA and the Space Shuttle.

If you've ever watched the Space Shuttle land, bringing our hero astronauts safely back to earth, you'll be able to appreciate more what we were about to do. The Space Shuttle is pretty efficient in outer space, but after reentering the earth's atmosphere, its shape is not the most stable of designs. At least not at the slower speeds required to land the beast.

What they do is deploy a high-speed parachute to stabilize the big machine while on their final approach to the runway. As big as the Space Shuttle is, they actually have the same parameters as we do. The most efficient shape of the back of a wing is to taper all the way to a point. This takes away crucial space that could be used for necessary things. Things such as backup parachutes.

But that didn't stop them. They designed around it. What they came up with was a dual-stage parachute. After the high-speed chute is deployed and the big white bird touches down, the main parachute is deployed. It is actually just a continuation of the first chute. A second release is activated and now the high-speed parachute does double duty as a pilot chute to drag "Big Bertha" out for some serious stopping power.

Two parachutes, one canister. Our boys proved that you really could fit 10 pounds of shit in a 5-pound bag.

Chapter Nine
The Dog and Pony Show

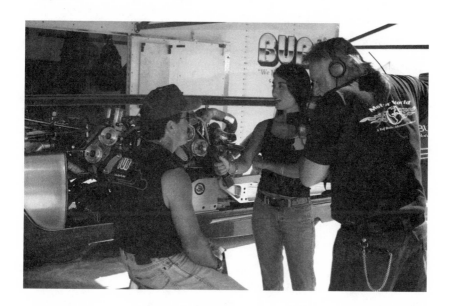

Whenever we go on the road to a show or an event where we are going to display the streamliner, we talk to the press. We call it our dog and pony show. We bring all the usual fluff: posters, revolving videos, and various promotional items. Because we run a business that ties into the performance aspect of what we do, if we can get in a good plug for BUB Enterprises, we're not above doing that either.

One such venue that we were asked to attend was the Indianapolis Motorcycle and Powersports Convention. This is an annual event and the biggest dealer show in the nation. Fred Fox,

One of many TV interviews done at the salt flats. *Photo courtesy of Larry Bliss*

who owns Drag Specialties (a distributor of our products and a major sponsor), asked us to come and to bring the racer along to see what kind of effect it would have on the crowd. This would be the first public display of our mighty machine.

The event drew in literally thousands of dealers, customers, and enthusiasts. We had the streamliner set up at the entrance to the Drag Specialties booth, with racks of our product on display all around it. The Drag booth was one of, if not the biggest, booths in the entire convention. That, along with a few other major companies Fred owns such as Parts Unlimited and Thor, took up nearly a small city block. As a manufacturer of aftermarket motorcycle exhausts, we thought this would be a great opportunity to talk to people about our product and have a little fun with them bench racing and playing show-and-tell with the streamliner.

To be totally honest, I don't think anyone even noticed our pipes. They would lean against our display racks, trying to get a closer look at the racer. It was a total babe magnet, too! Women would come over and be mesmerized by its long, sleek shape. They would rub their hands across its smooth glossy finish. Some would ask to sit in it. Others wanted to know who was crazy enough to drive it. They would come over and give me hugs and wish me well, like they were seeing me for the first and last time. And they all wanted their picture taken standing next to it. If I only had one of these things when I was in high school! It was incredible . . .

Oh yeah, and the guys loved it, too. No big news there. What *was* noteworthy was that it drew in some pretty important people who just had to have a closer look. One in particular was Malcolm Smith, a legend in the motorcycle industry who Denis actually knew and introduced me to. The man won eight gold medals competing in the International Six Day Trials and became one of the most recognized motorcyclists of his time after co-starring alongside Steve McQueen and Mert Lawill in the motorcycle classic, *On Any Sunday*. I was stoked! Almost everyone who passed through the turnstiles made the trek to the Drag booth to pay us a visit.

When the event came to an end, Fred, Denis, and I were standing around having a beer, when we noticed a peculiar sight. The carpet in front of the streamliner was actually worn out. The carpet fibers were worn away to the mat along the entire circumference of the streamliner. So much traffic had shuffled through to see the peculiar race machine that the industrial-grade carpet was literally worn away.

In Flat Rock, North Carolina, we had the whole rig on display. The race trailer, the bike, and all our gear. And our motorcycle exhausts. The event was called NVP, the National Vendors Presentation, and was created to allow all of Drag Specialties and Parts Unlimited's sales reps to see their vendor's wares and learn what made their part special and any tips they had to help them better sell their products.

This time we insisted on talking shop, but for a treat, on occasion we would fire up the bike. It was sitting on two heavy-duty stands which held it about 3 feet off the ground so it was easier to work on and much more visible.

Our trailer at the time was a specially designed rolling showcase. One whole side opened up and the wall became an enormous canopy, blocking out the sun's rays. At one point I had several of the sales reps inside the trailer checking out our goods when Denis fired up the bike. When it first fires, raw methanol gas occasionally spews from the motor, which burned our eyes and had us running for cover. The sound echoed from the aluminum trailer walls, stopping everyone in their tracks. Of the hundreds of vendors trying to spend quality time with their respective representatives, all eyes and ears were once again on us. If the boys with the coolest toys ruled the day, Flat Rock had just become our kingdom.

There were many other events where we displayed the bike or gave presentations. The Towe Auto Museum in Sacramento had several vintage race cars on display, and had decided to do a tribute to Bonneville Land Speed Record machines. They contacted Denis and asked if he would be interested in displaying *Tenacious II* alongside a host of other salt lake racers for the next six weeks. Denis agreed and asked if they would be interested in viewing the new machine during the inaugural open house. The bike wasn't complete—more a work in progress—but they were happy to have it and told him to bring it along for the open house.

When we arrived, the press went nuts. It was by far the most sophisticated salt racer they had seen. The carbon fiber monocoque chassis was state of the art. The on-board data retrieval system reeked of sophistication. The fighter-jet controls and digital read-out was something more commonplace in exotic military defense vehicles that traveled in excess of mach 1.

After a brief presentation welcoming the public to the museum's new display, Denis and a handful of other builders got a chance to address all who attended and to field questions. When it was over, a huge crowd quickly gathered around our new machine. Everyone wanted a closer look to see what a 350-mph speed racer looked like from inside the cockpit. I was asked to climb inside and explain the *whats* and *whys* of it all. It was a good time and a unique learning experience for many.

* * *

All the shows and events were fine, but the one that stands out above the rest happened at an elementary school in my hometown. My stepson-to-be had told me that his teacher posted pictures of race cars and motorcycles on one of her bulletin boards. There were also some pictures of our streamliner with the crew standing behind it, and one of me in it. He told his classmates that I was going to be his stepdad one of these days. They all liked the pictures and thought it was pretty cool that Mario's dad-to-be was a big-time racer.

The pictures were out of the local paper. His teacher, Mrs. Connel, had no idea anyone in her class knew any of her pin-ups. When Mario proudly told her who I was, she wanted to know if I would be interested in paying a visit to her class.

I agreed and a date was set. I'd never addressed a classroom full of 10-year-olds before, and for some reason I was more nervous than usual. When I showed up, Mrs. Connel called in a second classroom to join in on the presentation. Visions of *Kindergarten Cop* polluted my brain . . .

I decided to try to make my visit both entertaining and to enforce some sort of positive message. A few props would be in order, so I brought some of my protective gear: my helmet, the fireproof Nomex liner, my fire retardant racing suit and, of course, my matching fireproof shoes.

I also wanted them to get a taste of the racing experience, so I brought along a 10-minute promotional video which showed various runs we made at Bonneville, along with some narration by both Denis and myself. On top of that, I brought some samples of carbon fiber and Kevlar so they could see what the new bike was being made of. As I passed them around, I mentioned that the bulletproof vests police officers wear are made of the same material. The room filled with "oohs" and "ahhs." We had reached a new level of coolness.

After they watched the video, their little minds were filled with questions. They made me feel so at home that my prerace jitters had vanished. Everyone got into the act. Even the girls, who I was afraid would be bored, raised their hands and fired away. I expected my little dog and pony show to last about 30–40 minutes. About an hour and a half later we were finally wrapping things up.

When I left, I felt really good about the way things had gone. I expressed the seriousness of taking all the proper safety precautions.

We talked about all the training involved, the testing, and inherent danger. It wasn't like they could go home that night and take mom and dad's streamliner out of the garage and go 300 mph, but there were still concerns nonetheless. I also felt good for Mario who, at least on this day, was too cool for school.

* * *

One of the neat things about writing this book is that I get to take those of you who are into this sort of thing along for the ride. As you are reading this, it is "real time." I started writing this book about a year after we returned from our final running of *Tenacious II* in Australia in March of 2000. The building of the new bike is ongoing and being told to you pretty much as it happens. Same with the testing which, at this point, has yet to happen. To give you a timeline of sorts, as I sit here at the keyboard, it is February 25, 2003, at about 8 p.m. We have already reserved "private time" from the Bureau of Land Management (BLM) to run at Bonneville later this summer, with the first test session scheduled for the first week in July.

The new bike, which I fondly refer to as *Big Red*, is the seventh streamliner Denis has designed. It has already been put together and taken apart at least a dozen times. The transmission is currently in pieces being inspected and improved upon. The motors (we have two this year) are being built and prepped and readied for the dyno. The new front end is still under construction, and the much scrutinized dual-stage parachute design has yet to see the light of day.

Add to that the fact that a major sponsorship deal is currently being investigated; I have a new girlfriend (Tricia, Mario's mom), who just might be crazier than me; and in only four short months all of this will be put to the test, and you can get a pretty good picture of what's going through my mind at this very moment.

* * *

In keeping with current events, a sad thing happened only a short while ago with the passing of Don Vesco. By the time this book reaches publication this will be old news, but Don was a special guy and one who deserves mention. Anyone involved in racing at the salt flats has undoubtedly heard his name.

I met him several years back when he was doing some initial testing with *Turbinator*, his gas-powered, turbine-engined streamlined car. He and his crew had showed up late after pulling an all-nighter to ready his new machine for its first romp on the salt.

When they showed up, they quickly unveiled the new machine and hoisted it on to jack stands to get all four wheels off the ground. The car was impressive. Long, sleek, and narrow, with more horsepower than they could ever use. As of this writing, he and this machine have yet to be equaled on the salt, having run through the lights at 459.021 mph, establishing a new land speed record for gas turbine engines. Defeating Donald Campbell's record of 403.135 mph, Vesco set a new International Land Speed Record (FIA) for wheel-driven vehicles raising the mark to 458.44 mph.

Remember, on this particular trip *Turbinator* was still in its early stages. Once the big machine was elevated so the wheels could spin freely, he fired up the sleeping beast. A funny thing happened next as he engaged the transmission. The rear wheels began to spin in a forward direction as expected, but the front wheels (*Turbinator* is four-wheel drive) began spinning in the opposite direction! It wasn't difficult to surmise that something was amiss . . .

Shaking his head in disbelief, Vesco knew his day was over. He let the engine keep running until it was at full operating temperature. With a large section of the bodywork removed you could see the huge turbine and the hot gases escaping at its rear. He had a deflector plate at the rear of the turbine, which shot this massive flame straight into the air. (I believe this was mostly for show.) His good-natured crew, with weenies and marshmallows in hand, ran behind the machine with straightened coat hangers held high in the air. I'm sure Vesco also holds the unofficial record for the world's fastest weenie roast.

Other more serious accomplishments to his credit include being the first person to drive a streamlined motorcycle at more than 250 mph, which he accomplished in 1970 with a two-way average speed of 251.924 mph. He did this in a motorcycle streamliner powered by twin Yamaha 350-cc engines. In September of 1975, Vesco was also the first motorcyclist to exceed 300 mph. He set an American Motorcycle Association (AMA) record of 303.812 using two TZ750 Yamaha motors as the powerplant churning out more than 240 horsepower. *Silver Bird*, the name given to the Yamaha-powered streamliner, was the class of the field.

Never one to be satisfied, Don Vesco came back yet again with a new streamliner powered by twin KZ1000 Kawasaki engines and set the mark at 318.598 mph, a record that stood for nearly two decades. *Lightning Bolt*, the Kawasaki streamliner, also holds claim to the official one-way run top speed of 333.117 mph. At least at this stage, no one has gone faster in a legitimate two-wheeled streamlined motorcycle.

In 1999, Mr. Vesco was inducted into the AMA Hall of Fame for his many two-wheeled accomplishments. One of the things I admired most about the man was that he always believed no matter how fast he went, or what record he had broken, there was always room to do better. Don left behind some unfinished business. His most recent goal was to be the first to break the 500-mph mark. He and his turbine-powered streamlined car were almost a shoo-in given his most recent accomplishments on the salt with *Turbinator*.

As was always the case with Mr. Vesco, this still wouldn't be enough. His dream was to hold both the fastest wheel-driven car record (which he had already accomplished) but taken to another level at 500 mph, *and* regain the two-wheel record for motorcycles.

Lofty goals, but not impossible for a man whose entire mission in life was to constantly raise the bar and set new standards in the world of land speed racing.

Don died on December 16, 2002, after losing a battle with cancer at the age of 63. I will always remember him for his never-say-die attitude, the incredible toys he built and raced (with the help of his brother Rick), and his uncanny ability to push the envelope in speed racing to new levels. He was a great pioneer of our sport, and one who will not be forgotten.

Chapter Ten
"Let The Games Begin"

The September deadline for the bike's first test came and went without us making it out of the garage. There was simply too much still to do and not enough time. Our next window would be October 3 through October 5.

Things were coming together, but at a pace that was painfully slow. New Ohlins shocks were installed as the Penske units from the old bike wouldn't do. The old front wheel returned to the lineup and was fitted in place temporarily. My helmet had to be wired for sound, and a trick miniature microphone installed in place. Jeff

The only purpose-built motorcycle streamliner motor that I know of. It was designed by Joe Harrelson. *Photo courtesy of Gene Koch*

Boyle and Richard Miller, a new member to the team, worked their magic with the radios and in no time we had full communication between bike and crew. This was a first for our team.

Getting the new engine to run proved challenging. As plans were being made for hotel accommodations and the like, the party came to a stop—the engine refused to run.

The dyno room at RPM, Richard Farmer's famous race headquarters, was now ground zero. The crew gathered around as pull after pull brought little to no life from the V-4 powerplant. The engine was getting spark, and fuel was being dumped into the cylinders. Yet the motor refused to light.

Hours turned into days and we were faced with the very real possibility of missing our next window of opportunity on the salt. Denis pulled a few strings and was able to push our deadline back a few more days. We now had until October 10 to get our butts out there.

On Monday night, around ten o'clock, the mighty beast finally took its first breath. Apparently there was an issue with a timing gear that threw everything out of sync. Once the gear was replaced, everything was rosy.

Time was running out. Rather than go through the proper break-in procedures, or even spend a little time tuning the motor, a couple of quick pulls were made and the motor was yanked from the dyno and readied for installation into the bike. At 7,000 rpm the motor made a little over 385 horsepower. They didn't want to run the motor any harder than that, as it had yet to be properly broken in.

The numbers were promising. On the salt we usually run up to 8,500 rpm, and on the original motor that equated to around 420 horsepower. Its new sibling appeared to have all that and more. Only time would tell . . .

The new plan was for Denis and John to put the motor in the bike the following morning, and for the gang to meet and load up somewhere around midday. As was the current trend, day turned to night and it was now Wednesday morning. Pretty much all that was left was for Denis and John to put the bike on the ground, adjust the ride height, and fine-tune the alignment.

As it turned out, the ride height was way off. The rear shocks would have to be preloaded to raise the rear end. No easy feat on a streamlined bike as sophisticated as ours. The tail section and rear wheel had to once again be removed to accomplish this.

While the motor was being run on the dyno they experienced a water leak from one of the carbon fiber tanks. It was so small they decided to deal with it later. But now, with everything mounted permanently into the chassis, the leak had grown and was dripping water onto the floor. The jewelry-like carbon fiber tanks that took months to build were questionable at best.

Afternoon came and we finally got the call to show up to load the trailer. I noticed the water trickling slowly from the bike and asked John if they had started the motor in the chassis.

"There isn't enough time," was the official reply.

My concern was that the leak might get worse from vibration, and no one knew whether the composite chassis design would help absorb the vibration of the engine or enhance the effect.

We loaded our gear and finally hit the road a little before seven o'clock. Jeff Boyle, our resident "electrical wizard," was unable to make the trip. It was a little unnerving leaving one of our key players behind. With a full moon lighting our way, we pressed on, arriving in Wendover at two in the morning.

The next morning started with confusion and uncertainty. Having spent the entire previous night pounding the pavement, there was little time for a game plan or strategy. We thought we would awake to an early phone call from Denis telling us to meet at the buffet for a quick bite and the usual "rules of engagement," but the phone never rang.

Instead we woke up late and left for some grub. At the buffet where we expected to see familiar faces, all we saw was greasy food and an elderly gentleman shouting "Keno!" falling upon deaf ears. Not a great beginning, but we were optimistic that things would be better once we reached the salt.

On this particular trip I was teamed up with Ken Draper and Don Eslinger for the ride from Grass Valley to Bonneville. This would be the first time either of them set foot on the flats. The short drive from the hotel to the famed Bonneville Salt Flats exit proved traumatic at best.

A little background on Mr. Draper is in order to paint the clearest picture possible. Ken is a former off-road racer and has a reputation for immaculate equipment and an orderly lifestyle. Everything has its place, and everything must be perfect—always.

When I met Ken, he had just signed on with our company to head up a new ATV line of exhaust systems. He had a few quads of his own, which he proudly brought in to begin initial testing of our new designs.

In my life of professional motorcycle racing, I keep my equipment clean and in top running condition. But next to Ken's off-road ATV machines, it was apparent that I fail miserably in the buff and fluff department. Not only could you eat off his equipment, when you were done your fork would have a brilliant chrome luster and your napkin would bear the fragrant aroma of Armour All and Turtle Wax.

Everything Ken owns is this way. His new F250 Turbo Diesel four-wheel-drive Ford pickup is no exception. From the chrome custom running boards to the oversized billet aluminum wheels with monster truck tires, this thing reeked of cleanliness and cool. There's the tinted receding sunroof. The glistening white paint. And, of course, the matching camper shell with sleek lines and tinted glass.

As we approached the exit, I was certain visions of corrosion and salty floor mats danced inside his head. He started asking questions as to the safety of the parking area at the end of the frontage road where he intended to end his journey. The original plan was to leave the truck there and hitch a ride with others from the crew onto the salt.

Richard Miller had been sent out to look for us in an old Ford van loaded to the hilt with everything from generators to ice chests and folding canopies. We crossed paths in front of a truck stop at the beginning of the frontage road. It was the last inhabited area between us and the moonlike surface that was our destiny.

Ken looked pale and not at all happy. He eyed the truck stop and wondered if it would be better to park his immaculate rig there or continue on to the end of the road, which bordered the chrome-corroding and paint-dulling harsh environment that was Bonneville. I have to admit, if I were in his shoes and faced with the same dilemma I'd have issues as well. Hell, I left my truck at home for that very reason.

We talked with Richard and eyed the insides of the van. Equipment and supplies were stacked to the ceiling. There was only one other seat, the passenger side, and a steel divider wall separating the cab from the cargo area. Boxes, coats, and other miscellaneous necessities lay in a heap between the two seats.

There was only one possible solution. We would comingle our stuff with theirs and pile into the van. A quick trip back to the hotel gave Ken the peace of mind he was longing for. With his truck left safely behind on solid paved ground, we crammed ourselves in among the heaps of equipment and pressed on.

At the end of the frontage road a large wooden sign welcomed everyone to the famed Bonneville Salt Flats. Peering over the dash from my comfy perch atop a heap of clothing and collapsing boxes, a less welcome sight also awaited.

Water.

From pavement's end, for at least a quarter-mile, we rolled slow-ly through 4 to 6 inches of standing water. On the north side, toward the mountains, a much larger lake had formed and was threatening to pay us a visit, should a heavy breeze or wind materialize.

I should mention that not all of our crew arrived in the tradi-tional, four-wheeled manner. Richard Farmer, our engine guru, and a close neighbor friend of his arrived on two brand new V-Rod Harley-Davidsons. Both had left at eleven at night and drove straight through. They managed to have their bikes trailered to the pit area by one of our crewmembers so as not to have to cross the corrosive salt water at the entrance to the lakebed.

Bikes like these are much better suited parked alongside the likes of Mr. Draper's rig back at the hotel. They figured as long as they didn't have to actually ride the bikes on the salt, and as long as there was a trailer to haul them back to the end of the frontage road, no harm, no foul.

Such brave souls were they.

When we arrived at the pit area, everyone seemed busy doing one thing or another. The trailer's canopy was up and the bike was parked proudly beneath it on a special stand that held the stream-liner 3 feet off the ground. This made working on the machine much easier, and for the most part kept everyone off their knees.

My job as always is to familiarize myself with the course and make sure it is laid out properly. I also inspect the course for fall-en debris and other unsafe objects that might have become embed-ded into the surface over time.

Other than a few rocks and a lead weight that I found at the 3-mile mark, the salt was in pretty good shape. Pete Davis, Buzzy, and Richard Miller came up a few days early to prepare the surface and install the markers. The drag used to groom the course was nowhere to be found, but luckily, it was smooth enough that it didn't matter.

Richard was in charge of the course markers, and in his defense he had little instruction on how to complete the task. The markers he made consisted of a cloth rectangular centerpiece attached to a PVC framework.

The course markers are bright red and stand out wonderfully against the white salt. At speed they line up like a picket fence. Through the flying mile they are a red blur, as is everything at 300 mph. The mile markers (white with large black numbers) designate the precise distance traveled.

All the markers are 5 feet tall and 3 feet wide. Holes are drilled into the salt and the legs of the frames fitted directly into the concrete-like surface. This is the only way to keep the markers in place, should strong winds develop. Even these efforts cannot match the power of Mother Nature. On more than one occasion the course markers have blown away overnight, playing hide-and-go-seek with our crew the following morning.

As I drove down the middle of the course, most of the markers were either blowing horizontally in the wind or had wound themselves around the PVC framework. The cloth centers were only attached at the top. A black stripe on either side of the course would have been much better. For one thing, there would be fewer obstacles to hit . . .

Instead, the red course markers were placed every tenth-mile as a kind of border. There were so many of them that I could live with them being only partially visible. As for the actual mile markers, these are crucial, and at speed I need these to identify where I am on the course for shift points, acceleration into the flying mile, and for stopping distance.

Going down the course I noticed the numbers were only visible on the left-hand side. The right side was blank; those numbers were facing in the opposite direction for the return run. They are posted on both sides for easy identification. We didn't have enough markers to finish the job so I asked Richard if they could at least tie or weight the bottoms of the mile markers to keep them from blowing horizontally. Once this was done, we decided it would be good enough for initial testing.

Things only got worse from there.

With the external starter attached to the motor, John squeezed the trigger and it clunked and chugged as the big V-4 motor began turning over. The electricity in the air was so thick you could cut it with a knife. All eyes were on John and our magnificent state-of-the-art racing machine. It's too bad none of that electricity could find its way into the motor. After several unsuccessful tries, the starter was disengaged and put away.

We had an electrical problem and our master electrician was 500 miles away.

Try as they might, no one on the crew knew the ins and outs of the complex wiring system the way its creator, Jeff Boyle, did. We reached him by cell phone but it was impossible to diagnose the problem over the airways. A spectator from the sidelines who was an electrical technician jumped in to lend a hand, but he too failed to find an answer.

Not wanting to give up, Denis decided while the electrical problem was being addressed we would lower the bike to the salt and check the balance of the machine. At worst we could get in a few dead engine tows to see how she handled. This didn't require a running engine and would have to be performed first anyway.

I climbed into the cockpit and sat back while the boys held the bike steady. Denis put a level on the front bulkhead and watched as they let the bike go. It fell to the left like a lead sinker. He stuffed bags of lead shot into the cockpit with me on the right side. It wasn't enough.

A gopher was sent to town in search of more lead shot. In the meantime, a couple of huge chunks of solid lead ingot were scrounged up that could be shaped and formed to be used as ballast. More and more weight was added before we started closing in on what was thought to be a neutral setting.

While all this was going on, another demon raised its ugly head. As I sat in the bike, I looked forward through the tinted glass at the course in front of me. The view was so distorted I knew we had a problem. At home I had mentioned it, but agreed it might look better out on the open salt and might not be a problem there.

Boy was I wrong. With all the other problems of the day, I decided to keep this one to myself until later. I figured I could do the dead engine tows, maybe, but when it came time to start making high-speed motorized passes, the windshield would have to be replaced. I knew this was something Denis and John didn't want to hear, but the visibility was so bad that it just wasn't safe.

The crew pressed on, everybody working their asses off with little success. Pete Davis brought along a bike he had just built entirely from accessory parts he had ordered out of the Drag Specialties catalog. This was the second bike he built this way. The first was dubbed the *Fat Book Flyer* (named after the popular accessory catalog), which was basically a highly modified Fat Boy. His current machine was loosely based on a "Bagger" design and had yet to be tested or named.

With 5 miles of groomed salt starving for attention, Pete fired up his new machine and made a few passes down the course. Everyone stopped what they were doing and watched as Pete barreled along, having the time of his life. It was neat to see him run, but made me all the more bummed that our machine had yet to take its first breath.

With our heads down, we returned to the streamliner and continued on, shooting in the dark for a possible fix.

The day would soon be coming to an end. Long shadows began to form as the first quarter of the moon arched against the salt's flat surface. We were no closer to getting the streamliner up and running now than we were when we first arrived.

Denis knew it was time to throw in the towel. He called us together for a quick meeting. Bonneville kicked our ass as much as he hated to admit it. The only question was what to do next. There was a lot of work to be done on the bike before we could come back for another attempt. He made mention of all the things that were wrong and what had to be done to correct them. It was then that I brought up the subject of the windshield and the poor visibility. As was expected, he wasn't pleased, but he took it all in stride.

We simply weren't ready.

The good news was we were able to at least identify the problems so we could work on correcting them when we got back home. The plan was to tear down camp and pack up the trailer. We would head for home the next day.

Even the simplest of plans can sometimes go terribly wrong.

The sun quickly fell and we found ourselves packing in the dark. Luckily we had a generator and floodlights. We sent a truck ahead, which trailered the two V-Rods back to the frontage road. The new street machines were still virgin rides, having never left the trailer and touched the salt's damaging surface. The plan was to drop off Richard and his neighbor so they could ride back to town. The truck and trailer would return to finish packing.

We became suspicious after an hour had passed and the vehicle had yet to return. Another vehicle was sent out to see what went wrong.

The Bonneville Salt Flats is a strange place at night. It is so big and flat that it is easy to lose one's way. Everything looks the same for miles and unless you can identify landmarks along the way, you could find yourself in a lot of trouble.

Such was the case for Mr. Jans' rig and the V-Rod boys.

As is so easy to do out there, a wrong turn was made by one of the newer members on the team who was sent to deliver our V-Rod boys to safety. He was trying to get to the frontage road and sort of lost his way. To add to the problem, the water that was backed up against the mountains was moving in at an incredible rate, with nearly a mile of standing water already spanning the edge of the frontage road working its way toward the rest of us.

The truck and trailer had become stuck in the thick slurry of salt and mud just off the beaten path. Had they gone straight for just another quarter-mile, they would have made it in on the hard packed salt without a problem.

The virgin steeds were now salt flat whores. Richard and his neighbor made the unwise decision to unload their bikes and try to ride them in. Keep in mind that they are still a way out, with at least an eighth-mile of standing water between them and the frontage road.

While Richard maneuvered slowly and steadily in the direction of the hard packed salt, which is the runoff from the frontage road, his neighbor took a more direct approach, trying to shortcut his way straight in. This choice proved to have unpleasant consequences, as the bike and rider found themselves tossed into the drink—another victim claimed.

A scream rang out as the good neighbor tried feverishly to upright his bike. Richard ran to his side and helped steady the machine while the two inched their way in. The poor guy was devastated, and rightfully so. A brand new $20,000 state-of-the-art cruiser, which led a pampered life until now, was covered head to toe in the nastiest, most abrasive, corrosive substance Utah had to offer.

Richard's bike hadn't gone unscathed, and he, too, was not a happy camper. Not to mention that poor John's truck and Pete's trailer remained buried in the salt and were slowly taking on water.

We all took our turn crossing the water safely to higher ground, with the exception of the van we rode in on that morning. As fate would have it, the radiator decided to let go, and we were forced to leave it behind until morning.

A couple of locals showed up and saw our motley crew gathered at the end of the road.

"Is someone in trouble?" they asked innocently enough. They'd seen this movie before and knew exactly what was going on. We told them our situation, and sure enough they offered a solution. "I've got a Snowcat that'll pull you out, no problem. Five hundred bucks."

Five hundred dollars. What a way to end the day. We really had no choice. Denis and John dug deep and made the deal. The two locals left, promising to return shortly with their equipment. Making good use of our downtime, we did the only honorable thing we could do. Everyone pitched in and a beer run was made to the local truck stop not far away.

It was amazing the good spirits everyone was in having considered what we'd all been through. We toasted our efforts and swore to return with a vengeance. As promised, the Snowcat showed up and plucked our rig from the salt. It was eleven o'clock at night when we finally got out of there.

Some days are better than others . . .

Chapter Eleven
A Cold Day In Hell

If nothing else, our last trip was a good learning experience. When we returned home, many changes were made to the streamliner that at least got us pointed in the right direction. For starters, the leaky carbon fiber water tank was replaced with an aluminum one. It was strong, lightweight, and probably much more durable. After hours of mental masturbation, Denis finally came to his senses (at least in my opinion) and decided to have all of the tanks remade from the same material.

In October of 2003 we arrived on the salt under freezing conditions. It was so cold the motor refused to run properly. *Photo courtesy of Gene Koch*

A biggy for me was the windshields. They were terrible. When I sat in the bike and gazed out to where white met blue along Bonneville's horizon, it was disturbingly clear something had to be done. The twisted and distorted view took away any confidence I could muster to ride the thing at anything above the legal speed limit. Luckily, Denis agreed they were a problem and decided to do something about it, pronto.

The shape of our front windshield is very sleek and long, not unlike that of a glider. Denis found someone who actually made glider windshields and asked if he could help us. Twenty-five hundred dollars later we had the most gorgeous, distortion-free, one-off custom windshields ever to grace the skin of a streamlined motorcycle.

Jim Moser, a local sign painter and all around craftsman, was offered the job of installing these beauties—in no small part because neither Denis nor John wanted to risk screwing them up. They were that nice, and that expensive. Jim did an awesome job, as he does with everything he touches, and the finished product was excellent. I have to give credit once again to Denis for seeing to it that only the best will do in our quest for the record.

It is now October 28, 2003. Our last chance to test the new bike is only a few days away. We will be running from October 31 through November 2, weather permitting. Weather permitting is key this time out. When we looked up the weather report in Wendover on the Internet, it wasn't very promising. The expected high for both Friday and Saturday was 39 degrees, with a low on Friday of 26. The good news was a heat wave was expected to roll in on Sunday, bumping the high to a sultry 43. Speedos would be optional.

A lot happened since the last time we packed our bags to head for the great white plains. On the business side, we opted out of the larger building we planned to inhabit with ideas of moving to greener pastures in a more business-friendly state. Workers' Compensation and the cost of real estate in California put us at a disadvantage with competing businesses in the Midwest. Nevada made sense financially but not ethically. I argued the point that money wasn't everything and that our little town was beautiful and had a lot to offer.

For me, there were many lakes to ski on in the summer. There were enormous granite slabs and rock formations to climb that were among some of the best anywhere. In the winter, Tahoe was just a short drive away. I was in my own little paradise. Nevada was just an oversized sandbox. Ask our kitty what she thinks of sandboxes. I, for one, wasn't thrilled with the idea.

And then there were the World Finals held at Bonneville while we were back home mending our wounds. Sam Wheeler, driving the Kawasaki-powered *E-Z-Hook* streamliner, went 308, then 310, and finally an unbelievable pass with an exit speed of more than 336 mph! This was not a world record because he was unable to make a return run, but that is the fastest one-way pass ever recorded by a streamlined motorcycle to date.

The bar had just been raised . . .

* * *

Trying to break the world land speed record on two wheels is a test of many things. Some are obvious. Experience, equipment, talent, and skill usually top the list.

Sometimes it goes way beyond that.

Unfortunately, as the project grew, so did the possibilities. What happens after we get the record? The book deals, promotional and marketing potential. A world tour.

Money in certain peoples' pockets.

What started out as a group of guys working together toward a common goal somehow lost its innocence. The pressure was on to perform, and we all knew that. We had what it takes. It was only a matter of time. If only it were really that simple.

The afternoon we were to load up the bike and leave for the final test session of the 2003 season changed all that.

One of the arrangements Denis and I have provides a balance between the business world and the racing world we share. As the vice president and general manager of BUB Enterprises, I run the production end of the company and handle many of the day-to-day operations. There are other key players, such as Don Eslinger and Ken Draper, who also contribute enormously to the company's success.

Having a dependable team buys you many things. In this case, it buys Denis the time needed to work side-by-side with John Jans on the racer. John has Howard Carte to tend to his company's day-to-day needs while he spins wrenches and machines beautiful parts out of chunks of aluminum and steel. John probably has more hours into the actual building of the machine than Denis.

Howard and I go way back, spending many afternoons after work on the lake water-skiing and boarding, and sucking down way too many adult beverages. He's also responsible for some of the worst hangovers I've ever suffered in my entire life.

On this particular afternoon I'm in my office trying to tie up some loose ends before leaving to help the crew in loading up the bike and gear for our final test session at Bonneville. I'd only recently heard that Jack Dolan would be on the salt laying out the flying mile and installing the timing lights.

Apparently he was called out there for two reasons: First, the new catalog bike that Pete built needed verification of how fast it could go so that Drag Specialties could have bragging rights in their advertisements should he cut a fast time.

And second, we had yet to go after sponsorship for the streamliner. If in this session we could go, say, 300 mph, that would go a long way in securing some big bucks for our assault on the record. Trips to Utah and Australia were expensive. A little corporate help could make life a lot easier for Denis and the crew. Keep in mind we had yet to make a motorized pass on the salt with the new machine . . .

Some of the colorful vehicles running during Speed Week.

Photos courtesy of Ed Chamberlain

Ed Mabry's potent twin engine Triumph prepares for a run during Speed Week.

Photo courtesy of Ed Chamberlain

My brother (Bud Robinson) making a low fly-by before landing on the salt.

Photo courtesy of Ed Chamberlain

My former ride, Big Red. *Photo courtesy of Ed Chamberlain*

This shot is from the 2004 International Motorcycle Speed Trials. The entire pit area was under water when we arrived. The track wasn't much better.
Photo courtesy of Gene Koch

This is from my last run in Big Red on private time in 2004. Look close and you can see that underneath the shell, the bike is on fire. Seconds later the rear tire would explode sending carbon fiber body parts flying in every direction.

Photo courtesy of Gene Koch

It took all the fire extinguishers we had to put out the fire. Big Red was dead.

Photo courtesy of Gene Koch

A few seconds earlier I was strapped inside. Thank God for Buzzy and Howard who saved my hide. *Photo courtesy Gene Koch*

The *EZ-Hook* Streamliner. *Photo courtesy of Meggan Bechtol*

Mike Akatiff works on the bike he created, the *Top-1 Ack Attack* streamliner.
Photo courtesy of Nathan Allred, Treasure Photography

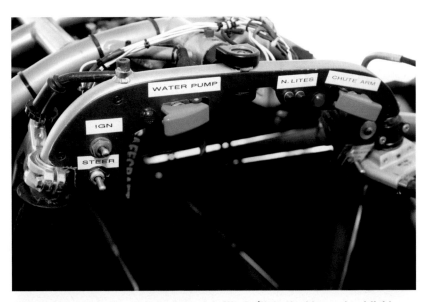

The controls inside the cockpit of the *Ack Attack*. (Note the blue and red lights. Blue indicates excessive wheelspin; red indicates the front end is lifting.) Like any true motorcycle, the main controls attach to a pair of handlebars.
Photo courtesy of Nathan Allred, Treasure Photography

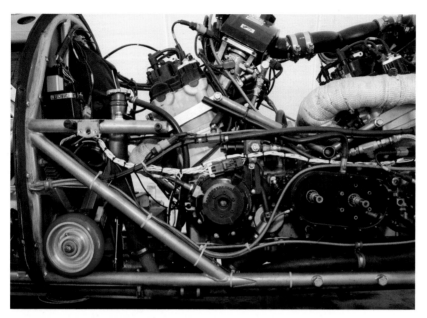

Two turbocharged Suzuki Hyabusa motors power the *Top-1 Ack Attack*.
Photo courtesy of Nathan Allred, Treasure Photography

Our original test session held at Silver Springs Airport in Nevada.
Photo courtesy of Tricia Robinson

This was the first time I climbed inside the cockpit of the *Ack Attack* streamliner. It was love at first sight! *Photo courtesy of Tricia Robinson*

The *Top-1 Ack Attack* racing team. *Photo courtesy of Nathan Allred, Treasure Photography*

One of the few great speed shots. Those are our pits blurred in the background.
Photo courtesy of D&W Images

This is the push bar Mike designed. It attaches at the rear of the *Ack Attack* and keeps us intact before I engage the transmission and pull away.
Photo courtesy of Ed Chamberlain

The onboard cameras had to be manually plugged in before each run.

Photo courtesy of Bart Madson, MotorcycleUSA.com

Moments before making our return run and setting a new world record.

Photo courtesy of Bart Madson

The calm before the storm. This is the cockpit lid to the *Ack Attack* resting against a Top Oil umbrella at the end of a long day of racing. *Photo courtesy of Meggan Bechtol*

Victory. *Photo courtesy of Grant Parsons, American Motorcyclist Association*

Bart Madson of MotorcycleUSA.com interviews me on the run.
Photo courtesy of Meggan Bechtol

On top of the world. This was taken after our record return run after the crew
and the rest of the media caught up with us. *Photo courtesy of Meggan Bechtol*

Shortly after our record run, Dave Despain did a live interview with myself and Denis Manning via satellite that aired on his Wind Tunnel show on Speed TV that afternoon. *Photo courtesy of Meggan Bechtol*

Sam Wheeler, Dave Campos, and myself. Three of the fastest men on two wheels. *Photo courtesy of Ed Chamberlain*

Mike, Christy, and Gregg Akatiff. *Photo courtesy of Nathan Allred, Treasure Photography*

Chris Carr and I compare notes in the *Top-1 Ack Attack* pits.

Photo courtesy of Jean Turner

Cooling it with friends and family. *Photo courtesy of Tricia Robinson*

Mike Akatiff watches as Chris Carr makes his first fast. We were all surprised when they announced his time. *Photo courtesy of Meggan Bechtol*

My son Mario and I sharing a break in the action. *Photo courtesy of Tricia Robinson*

Best seat in the house! *Photo courtesy of Ed Chamberlain*

So in walks this stranger whom I'd never met, nor was I expecting to see. He is directed to my office with briefcase in hand. Now, I've got nothing personal against lawyers; Tricia's sister is married to one and he's pretty cool. But this guy is here to see me the day before I am supposed to travel to Bonneville to put my ass on the line, about signing some papers he's drawn up that basically state that I'm uninsured and that my name, likeness, and photographs of me dealing with our racing program are the exclusive property of Denis Manning. If there are any profits to be made by anything having to do with our racing efforts, they belonged to him.

The innocence was over. This was about money. This was about covering one's ass. I was no longer an employee of BUB Enterprises while racing the bike. I was now a private contractor, self-employed, doing a job for BUB Racing.

No more workers' compensation. No more medical benefits. I was on my own. Not even the AMA's insurance coverage would be in place. If I wanted to be covered for this event, it would be up to me to find coverage—and I had two whole days to get it.

In Denis's defense, I understood what he was trying to do. My racing the bike under the employ of BUB Enterprises could feasibly put his company in jeopardy. Should I become injured or even killed, it did lend a certain amount of risk. BUB Racing wasn't the multimillion-dollar corporation that BUB Enterprises is now. You couldn't squeeze blood from a turnip and BUB Racing could be found in the produce section.

The part about exclusive rights to everything having to pertain to me was pure bullshit. If you are reading this book, it is only because I refused to sign the original contract.

I had to do a little legal investigating of my own, and a quick phone call to Tricia's brother-in-law, Brad, confirmed my gut feeling that I shouldn't sign anything until someone with my own best interests at heart could have a closer look.

I showed up at John's shop, where the bike was being prepared to be loaded, and stomped across the parking lot in search of the enemy. Howard and a few of the crew members were already there lending a hand loading the trailer when they noticed my disposition.

All stayed clear.

Denis met me at the door and led me out and away from the others where we could talk in private and not be heard. He asked if I had signed the papers. "I can't sign these," I argued. I'd share the rest but there's really no point to it. The bottom line is we reached a tentative agreement that we both could live with for this one meet. There'd be time later to argue over who got what and why. The salt was calling and winter was fast approaching. We packed our gear and headed east.

* * *

From the get-go, things were less than perfect. I brought my family along for their first trip, opting to take our four-wheel-drive SUV in case road conditions proved treacherous. We have a Honda Pilot, which is a pretty good all-weather family cruiser. Tricia and I handled the driving chores while our kids, Kristin and Mario, lounged in the back watching movies in full stereo sound from the fold-down DVD player, while munching on Halloween candy.

The farther east we went, the worse the conditions. Snow and rain, and even hail took turns playing with our nerves. Halfway across Nevada I glanced at the temperature gauge and saw it was 26 degrees. The closer to the Utah border, the more snow we saw.

As we crested the final hill leading to Wendover, the sky turned blue and for the first time in nearly a hundred miles you could see the sun. And the temperature had climbed to a promising 33 degrees. It ain't over till the fat lady sings . . .

We checked in and one by one the rest of the crew showed up, weathered but not beaten. Those who had come earlier to prepare the course also wandered in, though they looked a little less fresh, and a little beat up. Actually, they looked like hell.

Denis, Pete, Buzzy, and Richard Miller, and a new addition to our team, Kevin Kondra, all swaggered in, knuckles dragging, with red faces that were windburned and in need of a shave. They found their place at the bar and waited for the rest of our motley crew to arrive.

The game plan was made and the huddle was broken. All hands would meet on the salt at seven in the morning. We survived Mother Nature, but no one could guarantee we would survive the buffet. Thrill seekers at heart, the team gallantly threw caution to the wind, overcoming heat lamps and MSG in the pursuit of a hot meal. Once again, tenacity prevailed.

The following morning was met with high winds and freezing cold temperatures. It was hard to leave the comfort of the heated casino hotel to face the harsh environment ahead. Luckily, when we finally reached the salt, the freezing temperature was still there, but the winds had already begun to die down.

There was still nearly a mile of standing water from the frontage road inland. The V-Rods stayed home, and we positioned light beacons along the way to ensure safe passage back to the tarmac.

Richard Farmer, our engine guru, brought along his commuter car—an older, near-death station wagon with wooden side panels. He said if it broke down out here, he would just leave it. This car immediately became the favorite choice for running errands and making passes down the salt. While the crew prepared the bike and made some last-minute adjustments to the mile markers, I borrowed the trusty steed and went out to examine the course.

Everybody has their job to do, and mine is to become familiar with every bump, pothole, and rut that could put me in danger while running at speed. It's hard enough to maneuver a 24-foot rolling missile through crosswinds and the like. Throw in a few speed bumps and crevices, and it can get ugly real quick. Knowing where these obstacles are in relation to the course markers can mean the difference between a good day and one you'd rather not talk about. Luckily, other than a few rough spots where the salt had worn thin, it was in pretty good shape.

When I returned, the bike was already out and on its stand. It looked beautiful on the salt. It looked fast. Denis, who for the first time I was starting to have mixed feelings about, had already pulled the body panels and he and John were tinkering with the engine. They wanted to hear it run. We'd started it numerous times back home, but the new machine had yet to run on the salt.

This time when John engaged the starter the engine fired almost immediately. The sound was a bit mellower with the new exhaust design, but it still had plenty of authority. Smiles were pasted on everyone's frozen face. It took a while for the big V-4 to come up to operating temperature, but hell, it was only 36 degrees outside and I wasn't sure if I'd reached operating temperature yet. Little wafts of smoke puffed from the rear cylinder's exhaust stack that no one had noticed before. There were also unusual mechanical noises coming from the engine.

The frozen smiles became grimaces, the warm glow too short-lived.

They shut her down and took a closer look. Oil was seeping from the end of the exhaust pipes from the rear bank. The plugs were pulled and more oil was found. We weren't sure if the motor was already damaged, or if the extreme cold was just making things difficult. There was also concern that all the oil might have drained into the lower end during the long haul over, which could cause a hydraulic lockup of the crank. If you tried to force the motor to turn over, it could cause severe damage to a connecting rod or possibly a piston. If the damage wasn't already done, starting the motor again as more oil built up in the bottom end would be risky.

Instead, we decided to give the motor a rest while we did some initial tow testing. On the last trip we didn't get that far . . . our balance was off and the windshield was too screwed up. We thought those issues had been addressed this time.

After donning my race suit I felt warm and fuzzy all over—literally. This was one of the few times that my inch-thick, fire-retardant, one-piece, top-fuel racing outfit felt almost comfortable. Aside from the 10 pounds of Nomex and other unburnable crap that goes into the making of one of these walking mattresses, it was kind of nice. I was the only warm person on the salt.

This was a full dress rehearsal, so after installing my earplugs, helmet, and gloves, I crawled into the cockpit and plugged in my radio equipment while John strapped me in. We did a couple of tests to see how the communication worked between myself and the rest of the crew.

When John was done, the canopy was put into place and fastened shut. I gazed out the new windshield as the tow strap was being fitted to the release mechanism in the nose of the bike. I was relieved to see the huge improvement over the last version. The odd shape would never be completely distortion free, but this was as good as it gets. I was happy.

Even though this would be a dead engine pass, every time the canopy is closed it's just you and the machine—loneliness creeps in beside you. What it all boils down to after all the hard work of the countless people responsible for getting you here is this: They're all on the outside looking in. It's an eerie feeling and one that's hard to describe.

Without the motor running, it's also amazingly quiet. You'd swear you could hear the blood pumping through your veins. You force short breaths of air in through your constricted lungs, your chest and shoulder straps so tight you can barely move. The rules say a neck collar must also be in place, and this cumbersome gadget limits head movement and adds to the "straightjacket" effect.

As I mentioned earlier in this book, comfort is not a primary concern when designing streamliners, where every added inch of space becomes added drag. The smaller and narrower the machine, the less wind drag against its surface.

John gives me the thumbs up and jumps inside the tow vehicle. Jeff Boyle is riding shotgun and operating the handheld radio. The slack is taken up and Boyle radios me to see if I'm ready. After confirmation, John pulls slowly away, but graduallie picks up speed as was prerehearsed before the run. This was the first time I sat in the new bike while it was in motion. It felt good to be finally under way, but only moments into the run something also felt terribly wrong.

The bike seemed to favor the left side, and no matter how much steering input I gave to counter the effect, there was just no overcoming the sensation. Technically speaking, something was out of whack. I decided to release from the tow vehicle before we built up too much speed. At about 45 mph I cut loose with the intention of just freewheeling down the course and bringing our first test run to an end smoothly and safely in the middle of the course.

What none of us realized was just how bad the problem was. When I hit the tow release, the bike made an abrupt left turn. I was headed for the sidelines and the only action left for me to take was to lean heavily on the brakes. It stopped easily enough, but not before reminding all of us that we still had a long ways to go before we would be ready for any record attempts.

Tow test No. 1: Top speed 45 mph—dead engine. Skids were never raised and the bike pulled hard left. No "attaboys" on this run.

The bike was put back on its stand and the nose removed so we could take a closer look inside. The most obvious problem was the new front wheel. It was way off center, hugging closely to the right-side fork.

Howard had pointed this out back home but was assured it wasn't a problem. This time he was taken more seriously. A while back Denis had purchased a theodolite for aligning the machine. A theodolite is a precision surveying instrument used for measuring angles with a rotating telescope. Marks were made on specific parts of the chassis and the theodolite was used to bring them into alignment.

Using this instrument, they were able to bring the front end of the bike within thirty-thousandths of an inch from where the rear was set. The problem was, these measurements had to be made with the front wheel off the bike and the front forks locked in a centralized position. No sophisticated aligning methods were used to guarantee the wheels themselves were within the same stringent tolerances. The fact that the front wheel wasn't centered in the front end was cause for concern.

The old front wheel (which had been run on *Tenacious II*) was quickly installed. It appeared to work better—at least *visually* it ran down the center of the forks.

The nose was reinstalled and the bike set back down on the salt. I climbed back inside and was strapped in place.

Tow Test No. 2: Top speed 55 mph—dead engine. The bike still pulled to the left, but not nearly as bad. A couple of times I was able to balance momentarily between the skids, but it would always end up favoring the left side. When I released from the tow vehicle the bike felt much better, only graduallie fading to the left side of the course. The skids remained down and the bike still pulled, but an "attaboy" was nearly in reach.

By now it was almost noon, and plans for lunch had to be made. Tricia, Richard Miller, Kristin, and Mario were elected to run into town for sandwiches. Richard Farmer's station wagon was commandeered for the mission. My two kids, Kristin, 15, and Mario, 12, had spent most of the morning behind the wheel running folks back and forth across the salt in the wood-paneled wonder at speeds up to 80 mph. They'd both driven faster than their old man so far, and were understandably unimpressed.

After a few minutes of arguing over who would get to drive till they reached pavement, the wood-paneled wonder made tracks for civilization and Subway sandwiches.

Meanwhile, we were constructing a game plan of our own. I asked John to run down the right side of the course. My thinking was, if I could release from the right side, I could use the entire course to maneuver and try to balance the machine with the skids up. This would be a crucial test, as the only way to tell if the bike would respond properly to my steering input was to get it off the skids. The safety net would be gone. Once the skids were up, if anything went wrong, I would crash.

In all my years of driving *Tenacious II*, I only crashed it once, and that was only because we were running during Speed Week and conditions were terrible for motorcycles, especially *streamlined* motorcycles. It had rained off and on and the course was wet and slick. I remember releasing from the tow vehicle and just starting to roll on the throttle. The rear wheel broke loose and spun the bike sideways. The next instant I was on the ground sliding sideways down the course.

That was my only crash in *Tenacious II* in three years of racing.

We had *Tenacious II* wired. I could raise the skids at only 20 mph while still being towed up to speed. I could also bring the bike to a complete stop with the skids still retracted. I proved this on video one time when the skids failed to deploy. The footage shows me bringing the bike to a complete stop with the skids still up.

What you can't see is me inside trying desperately to get the skids to deploy. The air rams had failed, and no matter how many times I hit the switch to lower them, they wouldn't budge. I balanced this 20-foot-long machine to a complete stop while lying on my back strapped inside, only to topple over once all forward motion had ceased.

There was perfect synchronization between driver and machine.

The bike was perfectly balanced and perfectly aligned. It reacted perfectly to my steering input and made my job much easier. I was also perfectly in tune with this machine. At the end of a high-speed run I could literally pull the bike up right beside the pit trailer and ease it over onto one of the skids and stop exactly where I wanted. All this after covering 8 to 10 miles of salt at speeds of up to nearly 300 mph and then throwing out the laundry and having 50 or 60 feet of parachutes dangling behind me. Everything had to be right to pull this off.

On *Tenacious II*, everything was.

So off we went, John towing me on the right side of the course as planned. The front wheel change meant I didn't have the benefit of a working speedometer on my electronic screen. The pickup magnet on the new wheel was in a different location, thus the sensor on the front fork failed to get a reading. I had Boyle announce to me the speed from the tow vehicle in 10-mph increments.

As we picked up speed I tried to find balance between the two skids. Each time I did, it was only momentary. The bike always ended up back on the left skid. I decided to leave the skids down until I released from the tow vehicle. This would be somewhere between 50 and 60 mph. Like I said, in *Tenacious II* they would be up only seconds into the run. It handled that well.

My reasoning for waiting was simple: If I lifted the skids while still attached to the tow vehicle and crashed, I would be dragged behind John and Jeff. Also, if they hit the brakes after the crash, I could end up in the cab with them, along with 24 feet of crumpled streamliner.

No, I'd take my chances once I was on my own . . .

30 . . . 40 . . . 50 . . . it was time. Somewhere between 50 and 60 mph I released. I waited until the tow vehicle was out of the way and I had the bike as neutral as possible. I hit the skid toggles (on this bike there are two), which retracted the skids. My first thought was how long it took for them to retract. What should

have been instantaneously was definitely not.

We knew going into this run that the batteries were weak due to the fact that the motor wouldn't be running. The skids on the new machine are run by electronic solenoids instead of air rams. A large battery was placed between my knees and duct tape was run across my legs in case of a crash to keep the battery hopefully in place.

Even with the extra battery power, the skids did not function properly. The moment I hit the skid toggles it was over. The bike pulled left before the skids were even fully retracted. I hoped that by steering left it would keep the bike upright, but even as I did the bike was already on its way down. It didn't react properly to steering input, and somewhere between 50 and 60 mph I took my second ride on my side skidding down the salt out of control.

The bike had rolled on its left side, and at one point I thought it might go completely upside down. Out of the left side windshield I could see the abrasive salt grinding above my shoulder. Thankfully the windshield and slick body surface stayed intact. The smooth outer shell sent me zipping along like I was on a giant Slip and Slide. When the bike finally stopped, I radioed to the crew that I was okay.

Tow Test No. 3: Top speed somewhere between 50 and 60 mph—skids retracted . . . sort of. Bike once again pulled to the left, but did not react properly to steering input. End result was the bike crashed on its left side.

I was only glad that Tricia and the kids were gone and didn't witness our little mishap. This sport was still all too new to her, and I didn't want her worrying needlessly. I was fine. It was the bike that needed attention.

On November 1, 2003, testing of the new machine for the season was now over. The rains and snow were building and the salt would be too wet to run on until the following summer. Officially, we would be docked one "attaboy" for our efforts.

Chapter Twelve
Crunch Time

There were a host of changes that once again had to be made before the new season. Unfortunately, we had a few obligations we needed to get out of the way before they could take place. Two of the biggest motorcycle accessory trade shows took place within two weeks of one another. The first was in Cincinnati, Ohio; the second would take place in Indianapolis at the RCA Dome pavilion.

Our sponsors requested the presence of the new machine at each of these events to show off to the public. That meant the bike would be gone for an entire month. We had to get busy.

Big Red with canopy removed. *Photo courtesy of Larry Bliss*

The first thing that had to be done was purely cosmetic. The bodywork on the left side of the machine was pretty much trashed from the spill. A little fresh paint and a lot of elbow grease had her looking like new in no time. The left side windshield was also scratched, but to my surprise they were able to rub it out and it looked good as new.

The bike was then outfitted with corporate logos with fancy lettering and striping. It's rumored that there was over $1,000 worth of actual gold leaf in the artwork. Buzzy told me if I crashed it again, he would pan the salt for gold—thanks for the vote of confidence, Buzz.

With the new paint and stickers in place, the bike was ready for show and tell. Denis hauled her to both Cincy and Indy, where the new bike was publicly debuted to the world. Cameras flashed and hands were shaken. Denis was in his element. We flew in to meet him and to participate in each event.

I have mixed emotions about working the shows with Denis whenever the streamliner is involved. I mean, I think it's great that everybody gets to see the bike and see how far technology has come in the way of motorcycling. Our machine is cutting edge stuff. And Denis is rightfully proud.

But . . .

Being the driver, many times I am asked what it's like to go 300 mph in such a wild machine. Most of these reporters have never traveled faster than their family car or weekend sportbike can go. They want to know what it feels like. They want to know what's going through your mind as you travel at unheard of speeds strapped in this torpedo-like contraption. They want to relive the experience through me. And I'm more than happy to share that with them.

If given the chance.

To be honest, I purposely avoid trying to share the limelight with Denis. It's *his* machine. He put together the team to create and build it. The sponsors, promotion, the travel . . . all Denis. And he lives for this stuff.

I recently overheard a TV interview with Donald Trump about success and business. What he basically said (not word for word) was that it takes a certain amount of "ego" to be successful. You have to believe in yourself and be willing to throw it out there. Denis has those qualities. My dad and my brother, for sure, share those same qualities. But Denis also demands recognition . . . he thrives on that part. And he deserves it. But it can make it difficult to get a word in edgewise whenever there's an audience.

I'm sure I have a bit of an ego, too. I don't think I could climb into our carbon fiber and Kevlar coffin and barrel down the salt only inches off the ground at inhuman speeds if I didn't believe I was capable of pulling it off. I've had my successes in racing, and that's partially why I was chosen for the job. But I'm not a show-man like Denis. I shy away from large crowds. It's his place to thump his chest and tell the grandiose story.

I'm content to be a piece of the puzzle. Besides, like I've said before, it's one hell of an "E" ticket ride only a select few will ever get to experience. I'm fortunate to have that opportunity.

When the bike returned from the shows it was time to get down to business. There was more testing to be done, parts to be improved on, designs that needed changing. Before the bike came apart Denis called the team together for a sort of dress rehearsal. He wanted to activate the fire extinguisher system and see how well it performed. It had spray nozzles in both the cockpit and the engine department, and he just wanted to make sure the system would be adequate in the event of an actual fire.

The old bike was equipped with Halon fire extinguishers. The way they worked when activated was by displacing the oxygen, a necessary ingredient for anything to burn. They were quite danger-ous in the fact that the driver needed oxygen to breathe. Remove that and you also remove one key to the driver's survival. Not good, in my opinion.

The new design was much safer. Compressed water was mixed with a fire retardant chemical. If the bottles were activated, the spray released from the nozzles resembled soapy water. It seemed like a much better choice, but until we actual tested the system, we could only hope it would be adequate for our needs.

Denis wanted someone sitting in the cockpit so we could see just how much coverage the driver was getting. The side panels were removed from the engine compartment so that during our dress rehearsal we could also monitor the coverage the motor was getting.

Enter our "splash test" dummy.

My good friend Buzzy actually volunteered for the job of climbing into the cockpit of the streamliner to weather the storm. Many thought I should be the one inside, but my reason for remaining on dry ground was to witness first-hand the efficiency, or inefficiency, of the new system. As it turned out, both compartments received adequate coverage. My only complaint was that the spray nozzle in the driver's compartment sprayed too high, showering the driver's helmet and shield with the sudsy liquid, which would make it difficult to see at 300-plus mph. Even if it were to put the fire out, the odds of a high-speed crash were greatly increased. Also not good, in my opinion . . .

We learned a lot from Buzzy's willingness to test the waters of our new device. A shroud would be built to better control the spray from the nozzle, hopefully keeping it just below the line of vision. I have to say, it was a memorable sight to see our man, Buzzy, dressed in a yellow PVC-coated raincoat, wearing a full-coverage face shield, behind the wheel of our machine. The optional oxygen bottle dangling from his lips was the finishing touch. Captain Safety had met his match. All hale the new Splash Test Dummy, Buzz Mulbach.

More testing was needed.

As you recall, the bike didn't want to go straight in our test runs. There were probably a number of things contributing to the problem. The front wheel wasn't centered properly and there was flex in the front end. The alignment was out of whack, and maybe the left turn indicator was left on. Anyway, a closer look was necessary to get to the heart of the problem.

As the bike came apart, problems started to surface. Even though we hadn't made a motorized pass, the three-piece billet aluminum swingarm assembly had worked loose and was showing signs of flexing. Denis and John worked on a stiffer center section design that would incorporate heavy dowel pins in the assembly for better rigidity and less stress on the bolts. John created a beefier carbon fiber rear fender that "boxed in" the swingarm spars and increased the strength of the entire assembly. And it looked cool.

Tests were made on the chassis to analyze its strengths and weaknesses. Some were scientific and done under the supervision of our design guru, Joe Harrelson, with the help of computer modeling and other high-tech gadgetry. Other "rear world" testing consisted of both Denis and Howard jumping on the bike and trying to register flex by throwing large amounts of "dead weight" at it to see if it would move. I'm told their combined weight of well over 450 pounds barely budged the rigid composite chassis. I wonder if the NASCAR boys use equally sophisticated methods when testing their latest designs.

The front end was next. The original design was an engineering marvel, infinitely adjustable but, unfortunately, prone to an infinite amount of misalignment problems. The same Heim joint/turnbuckle design that made it possible to adjust the front end in every direction was also responsible for some of the handling problems that we encountered on our last test session. Apparently there was excessive "flex" in the design, which hindered steering input and took away any "feel" one normally had with a permanently attached steering head. The old adage "if it ain't broke, don't fix it" came into play with Denis and John redesigning the steering head and opting for the more stationary, nonadjustable design used on conventional motorcycles. Denis's original design was not without merit, and I think a revised version of his adjustable design will probably resurface somewhere down the road. For now, we chose the path of the straight and narrow.

Things were progressing nicely, but believe it or not, time was already running short. As of today, it is Thursday, May 27, 2004. Our first scheduled test date this year is the Forth of July weekend, only about five weeks away. Yikes!

The other night I was asked if I'd suit up and climb inside the bike so the new front end could be adjusted. The steering controls felt a little cramped and were actually coming in contact with my knees at full lock. We considered moving the controls back, closer to my chest. The downside was we would need longer steering cables, and more importantly, it constricted my arm movement, which made it more difficult to maneuver.

A beautifully constructed carbon fiber seat pan with a rigid honeycomb center would need to be removed or at least modified if we wanted to avoid moving the steering controls. It held me a little over an inch off the cockpit floor, allowing a void for the control cables and wiring harnesses to pass through. I asked if it could be removed. They said no, but that it certainly could be modified to allow me to sit practically on the floor, give or take the thickness of a few wires and a few necessary cables. They would be routed directly down the center of the cockpit floor, and the floor panel would be contoured with a slight rise in the middle section for the hardware to pass through.

The new design would literally have me being "one" with the machine. Talk about utilizing every square inch of available space. The good news was they were happy to make the changes to get it right.

With only a little over two weeks left until we returned to the salt, the pace had become a little more hectic. Everyone on the team had projects to complete. Richard Miller was in charge of the course markers and also ordering my new race suit and all the non-flammable garb that goes with it—Nomex head sock, Nomex-lined gloves, neck brace with Nomex-impregnated foam, Nomex everything. Fire is a serious thing when you're driving an enclosed alcohol-burning racer.

Buzzy was in charge of building the drag we would be using to groom the course. This thing was monstrous, made of 8-inch-wide flanged I-beams designed to knock the high spots off the salt's crusty surface. Because Buzzy also ran our automation department at the shop, he was beginning to wonder if he would be able to make the trip to the salt when it was time. I assured him that we weren't leaving without him and that whether his robots were making parts or not, he was going to be with us on the salt.

Jeff Boyle was busy putting the finishing touches on the electrics while engine guru Richard Farmer was burning the midnight oil making sure our new motor was up to the task. No one can make an engine sing like Richard, and luckily for us, he was on our side.

On June 19, I stopped by the race shop to see how the crew was doing. The swingarm was still apart but the newly designed center section was nearing completion. The solid billet piece was a work of art. John and Howard spent countless hours designing and writing programs, and then an additional day and a half of actual machine time. The center section would replace a two-piece bolt-together unit that connected the two hefty swingarm spars. The new piece was at least 50 percent stronger and didn't add any significant weight to the rear of the bike.

The exciting news was that Richard Farmer was just about ready to start the motor. Even though the bike was only partially assembled, the motor could be run without the rear end intact. Howard plugged the laptop computer into the "brains" of the machine while John connected the external starter motor. At Richard's command they turned over the motor to prime the injectors, circulate oil, and to check the timing. After a couple of dry runs, it was time to bring the mighty V-4 to life.

Ear plugs were passed around and the doors were opened to the shop. A huge fan was turned on to help exhaust fumes exit the building. With fingers crossed, John once again triggered the starter. In seconds, *Medusa* fired and a deep rumble filled the air.

Hearing the familiar thundering pulse of our one-of-a-kind motor raises the hair on the back of my neck and gives me goose bumps every time I hear its roar. I have a certain connection with *Medusa*, the two of us having been through a lot together already, and now we're coming back to the party once again to settle unfinished business.

As the core temperature rose, a few quick raps of the throttle sent shivers down the entire crew's spine. The building shook as the angry growl echoed against its walls. You could actually feel the motor's heartbeat overpowering your own, like that of a drum solo being pounded out inches from where you stood. We were one step closer to our goal today, and I was a happy camper.

With one week left before our first test of the year, it was major crunch time. The crew busted their hump readying the machine and all our gear for the journey back to the great white plains. Every spare minute I had available found me either at the gym busting a sweat, or on the road riding the company's new Harley-Davidson Softail. Throwing around a heavy motorcycle on a twisty country road at speed did wonders for my self esteem—not to mention my balance and timing. With our deadline in sight, we would soon find out if all our hard work would pay off.

It's times like these that make life so wonderful. It's all about the journey.

Chapter Thirteen
Walking Before You Run

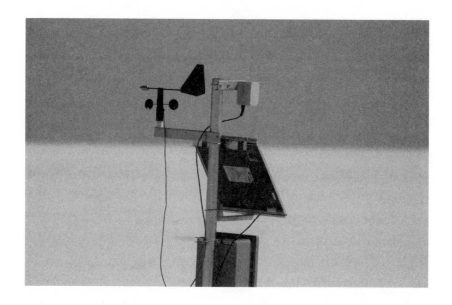

July 2, 2004. That's the day we arrived back on the salt to continue our quest. Actually, most of our crew had arrived several
days earlier to prepare the course. I'm fortunate in that my main
focus is only to drive and to be in shape to endure whatever is
thrown my way.

The trip was long and uneventful. We did make our annual stop
in Battle Mountain to purchase fireworks deemed illegal in the conser-
vative state of California. Mortars, huge bottle rockets, Roman candles,
all the good stuff. Things that go bang and shoot into the air are viewed

This is a wind meter. It not only tells you how fast the wind is moving, but also
from which direction. *Photo courtesy of Jean Turner*

as hazards in our heavily wooded state, but the vast desert sands of Nevada and the salty plains of Utah have little to burn. "Bring it on," they seem to say, almost invitingly. Who were we to disagree?

I had recently returned from a trip to Wisconsin, where we would be opening a new manufacturing facility for BUB Enterprises. We'd outgrown our confines back home and decided to set up a sister facility in the Midwest to take advantage of certain tax incentives and other money-saving opportunities. We would continue to grow out west, but Wisconsin was in the heart of big manufacturing, and our distributor's main headquarters just happened to be in the vicinity. Travel was becoming more frequent in my job description, and eight hours on the road to Bonneville did little to ease my traveling blues.

"The salt's the best I've ever seen," were the exact words Denis used when describing the conditions of the Bonneville course. It was encouraging, but somewhat hollow. You can ask anyone on the crew; Denis is like a broken record when it comes to describing the salt. His testimonial has a diarrheal quality—his eternal optimism leaving you with a feeling of warmth that one only hopes isn't a load of crap.

In his defense, the salt really was outstanding on this occasion. Pete and his crew did an amazing job with the course. Buzzy's new skid leveled and groomed the surface better than any of our previous efforts—and we had eight full miles of track to test on. We also had a slight side wind, which traveled right to left across the course at 3–5 mph.

I was buckled in while the tow vehicle lined up in front of me. Our goal was to make a pass and see if the changes we made were an improvement. If I could get the bike to balance between the skids and keep it pointed down the center of the course, that would be a welcome start. As it was, the bike did go straight, but it still favored the left skid. The new front end was much more responsive and actually had that "feel" that was missing from the earlier design. I could steer hard left and actually get the bike up off the skids, but it would always return to the left side. More work needed to be done.

In our world of high-tech, state-of-the-art equipment, it's funny how some of the most basic principles still apply. We had a balance issue that needed to be corrected. The fix: Throw some lead shot at the problem and see if it goes away. Denis filled a woven bag with nearly 20 pounds of the lead BBs and stuffed them in the driver's compartment just behind my right shoulder. We held the bike perfectly level and let go. It seemed to have near perfect balance. We taped the bag in place using another piece of high-tech ingenuity—duct tape.

Off we went again, the bike reacting better than before, but still favoring the left skid. I was determined not to raise the skids until we had a neutral machine. As we learned from our previous test session in October, this practice was extremely hard on the paint.

One factor we couldn't ignore was the wind. There was still a constant 3–5 mph breeze crossing the track right to left. We decided to turn the bike around and make a short pass in the opposite direction. With the wind now at our left side, we could see if we were battling more than just the proper amount of ballast.

John towed me up to about 40 mph. Right off I noticed an improvement in handling. I could balance the bike between the skids almost indefinitely. When I released from the tow vehicle, however, the annoying fall to the left skid returned. A brief meeting of the minds quickly followed.

It was my opinion that we still needed to add more weight to the right side of the bike. Even though I could balance the bike pretty good on this last run, the wind was partially responsible for this achievement. And at the end of the run, when I released from the tow vehicle and the bike returned to the left skid, it was only because the wind had died down, no longer offering additional support.

Six more pounds were added to the right side of the bike.

This time the right side body panel was removed and the additional six pounds were zip-tied to a steel strut above the fuel tank. We were all eager to get back out there and see if this was the final adjustment needed to put us on the straight and narrow. Unfortunately, the wind and rain had other ideas and decided to pay us a visit up close and personal.

The wind picked up to an amazing 35 mph! Our handheld wind meters were spinning so hard you'd swear the things were about to grenade. To make matters worse, the rain also joined in, in typical Bonneville fashion. Our day was done. We loaded the bike back in the trailer and tried to make good use of our time. The alignment was checked once again and found to be spot on. We would have to wait until the next day to continue our quest.

Most of the crew dined on the Friday night seafood buffet in the upscale Montego Bay Casino/Hotel. The new digs were pretty cool. I've stayed there on many occasions before when it was called the Silver Smith, but the newly renovated hotel offered better comfort and a more pleasant atmosphere than its predecessor. As for the reheated fish under heat lamps, well, it only gets so good . . .

Saturday, July 3. A much better day—or at least it started out to be. From the moment we arrived, it was obvious that the steady breeze and gusting winds were no longer with us. The course markers hung in limp formation, lifeless and still. Half the crew was still on the salt reinstalling the PVC-framed course markers that either blew away or crumbled under the gusting winds of the previous evening. I'm sure if Denis had used a painted black line like everyone else, this wouldn't have been a problem.

The other half tended to the bike in preparation for the first morning run.

The plan was for John to tow me up to 40 mph, where I would release and see if I could balance between the skids. We didn't want to go too fast in case the balance was still off. Too much speed with the skids still down presented problems of their own. The skids work fine up to about 35–40, but much faster and they are only in the way.

As it turned out, things felt really good right off. I released at 40 mph and balanced between the skids for over half a mile before finally redeploying the safety net. I eased her onto the right skid (which it wouldn't do before) and coasted to a stop. The final six pounds of ballast made all the difference.

Even though these were still only dead engine passes, with a new machine these were major hurdles you had to get over before you could even think of going fast. The next test would set the tone for the rest of the weekend. If all went right after I released from the tow vehicle I was to retract the skids and coast down the salt balancing on my own. We had the new front end, the swingarm had been revamped, and we had enough lead shot on board to supply the local gun club with ammo for a week.

On the other hand, last time we tried this maneuver, in October, we put her on her side and made red and black skid marks on the salt. But that was last time.

Another little trick we hadn't thought about since running the old bike was aligning the streamliner and the tow vehicle with the center of the course before taking off. It might not sound like much, but if the tow vehicle starts off to the side, he will be angling toward the center of the course and I have no choice but to follow. Starting off in a turn is a lot more difficult than starting off going straight. Especially if you are trying to balance a 24-foot-long motorcycle while lying on your back strapped in place with two joysticks in your hands in place of handlebars. Believe me, every little bit helps.

As it was, everything went well. As John built up speed, I radioed him to take me all the way to 50 mph. I was balanced perfectly between the skids when I released from John. So far, so good. I just coasted for a couple of seconds making sure everything felt right.

It was time.

You're probably thinking, "No big deal. At 50 mph, no worries." Well, like I said, last time we tried it the end result wasn't exactly what we were hoping for. Sure, body shops have to earn a living, too, but not necessarily at our expense. I wanted to be sure I could pull it off before taking away the safety net.

I was in the center of the course. The skids hadn't touched salt since long before I released from the tow vehicle. My vision was excellent. There was no wind and no rain in sight. I took a quick breath and triggered both toggles up, which retracted the skids. I could hear the skid doors slam shut as the light indicators told me that the safety net was gone. And you know what?

It was cake.

The thing just kept going straight. Sure, I had to give steering input to keep her steady, but that was always the case. It didn't favor the left over the right or wobble or do anything weird. I found myself in the zone, floating down the salt at just below 50 mph without a care in the world. The only sound was of the salt crushing underneath my Goodyear front and Mickey Thompson rear LSR tires. I coasted for nearly a mile before redeploying the skids. I think I toggled the skids down at around 35. In *Tenacious II*, I could easily go less than 20 mph and still be in control, but there was no need to push our luck. Not yet.

When *Big Red* finally came to a stop, I hit the microphone button on the left joystick and let out a celebratory yell. Thanks to our new VHF radios, everyone within a 5-mile radius got to hear me whooping it up. I was pumped and I wanted everybody to know it. It's not easy getting one of these bad boys to handle and they managed to pull it off. Our guys did a great job and I just wanted to share my enthusiasm. I had a smile painted on my face for a half-hour. We were living large.

One small problem did occur during the last run that had to be dealt with. Denis had upped the air pressure in the rear tires which made it sit wider on the rim. The smell of burnt rubber lingered around the bike after the last run, but I thought maybe it was just the brakes heating up a bit. As it turned out, it was the rear tire rubbing against the inside bodywork. Space is precious and everything is made to the tightest tolerances allowable.

Just for the record, my mom and Tricia had first noticed how tight the fit was between the bodywork and the tire and brought it to my attention. In all my wisdom I told them that it wasn't a problem. As the tire picked up speed, I bragged, centrifugal force would actually make the tire grow taller, making it narrower in the process. They had stuck their fingers in the tiny gap between the carbon fiber shell and the big Mickey Thompson tire. "Looks awfully close to me," they warned.

I wonder if Mario Andretti received advice from his mother or his fiancé before a big race. Geez . . .

Before the first motorized pass, Denis and John wanted to make sure everything was perfect. The right side skid seemed to be in a bind and didn't seem to retract properly. Also, on one occasion while the bike was sitting, it started to go up without being toggled. The bike nearly fell over but the crew caught it before the new paint took an unplanned abrasion test.

Off came the carbon side panels, exposing the internal workings of our streamlined racer. The water and fuel tanks were removed, as well as the oil tank to make room to access the retractable skid mechanism. When they were done massaging the right side skid, the rear wheel was also removed and the bodywork also massaged for added tire clearance. Mother and Tricia were right!

The fuel, oil, and water tanks were reinstalled, as was the rear wheel. Denis let out about 10 pounds of air from the rear tire for additional clearance. The body panels were put back in place and the bike was lowered from our in-trailer hoist to the ground. It was time for *Big Red*'s first motorized pass.

July 3, 12:45 p.m. That's the official time when rider and machine took to the salt with the motor running. I was pulled away with the motor in neutral, revving up the big V-4 on occasion just for fun. The bike towed well with the additional rotating mass actually making my job a little easier.

For some reason, when we got to 60 mph, I was trailing behind John slightly to his left. When I released, usually John would pull off to his left and I would steer slightly right and off we'd go. This time as I watched the tether bounce on the ground in front of me, John started to go left, but then corrected and went right after seeing my position on the course. I'm glad he did because I was using up valuable momentum and needed to get it in gear before losing too much speed.

When he was clear I squeezed the right side trigger (for the first time in the new bike's brief history) and felt the transmission engage. The bike lunged forward, which was odd to me since first gear at 60 mph should have been a neutral transition. As I rolled on the throttle, I could tell that something odd was happening. The motor seemed to chug and struggle to gain momentum. The more throttle I gave, the worse the situation became. After about a mile and a half of this I realized I needed to abort the run. At about 90 mph I hit the high-speed chute. The upper wedge in the tail of the bike jettisoned and the pilot chute filled with air, pulling out the bagged high-speed parachute. As the tether tightened the bag pulled away and the 18-inch ribboned chute opened, just as we had planned. Because this pint-sized air brake is designed to function at speeds upward of 250 mph, it had little effect in slowing down *Big Red* limping along at a mere 90.

Even though it wasn't needed, I also hit the main chute. Everything had to be tested. Besides, the new bike offered many challenges, and one was the new parachute deployment method.

As I mentioned earlier in the book, to achieve maximum efficiency (the least amount of aerodynamic drag) the tail of the bike needed to end at a point, not unlike the trailing edge of a wing on an airplane. This doesn't leave any space for the parachutes to exit from, since you need a sizable chamber for each chute to store and escape from freely. Our fix was to have parts of the tail section actually release from the bike, exposing the proper size cavity for the parachute to release from.

When I deploy a chute, the first thing that happens is an air ram jettisons the tail section directly behind the parachute cavity, which also forces the pilot chute into the open air. The pilot chute is then responsible for pulling the bagged parachute out of the cavity into open air. The bags act as a buffer, not allowing the parachute to open too fast. As the bag is pulled away from the parachute, it is forced to open more slowly, eliminating that ugly hit that can be damaging to both man and machine. Had Nolan White utilized this technology, he might still be with us today.

So, after deploying the second chute, the wedge of bodywork jettisoned as planned, and the tiny pilot chute caught a breath of moving air and tugged against the bagged main parachute. The main chute is much larger, about 6 feet in diameter, and needs greater force to drag it from its home inside the tail of the machine. On this run, the larger bagged chute failed to exit the cavity completely, and at the end of the run was still hanging from the tail of the machine. It could have been that there wasn't enough speed for the tiny pilot chute to do its job, or the bagged chute could have just hung up inside the bodywork. Whatever the case, it was the brakes that brought me to a stop, not the parachutes. "Brakes? We don't need no stinkin' brakes." Remember?

The bike was lifted once again onto the work stand. I briefed Denis and John on what I thought was happening. To me it felt like the bike was in high gear (fourth) instead of first, which wasn't an engine problem, but more of a shifting or transmission issue. We found that the wiring of the shifting buttons on my controls was reversed. As it turned out, I had actually shifted directly into fourth gear. The fact that the engine had enough power to keep from stalling while trying to pull 350-mph gearing from a release speed of only 60 mph is pretty impressive.

The repairs were quickly made and the bike set back on the ground and readied for another attack. We were all anxious to advance to the next level. We had a bike that now handled well and a motor that seemed to be running strong. The plan was to make a first gear pass. I was to run her to the 4-mile, hit the chutes, and bring her to a stop. We needed to collect data on the motor, on the handling under acceleration, and make sure the parachutes functioned properly. Richard Farmer, the engine guru, asked that I keep her between 6,000 and 7,000 rpm for the run.

It had been a while since I ran one of these things at speed (four years earlier, Lake Gairdner, Australia) and the sensation of speed that went along with it. All I can say is, "What a rush." I wish there was a better way to describe it to you.

With the game plan in place we towed away, the motor happily rumbling inside its modern-day exoskeleton. This time, when I released from the tow vehicle I was exactly where I was supposed to be, and John pulled off to the left as planned. I pulled the left shift trigger (the wiring was reversed back to normal) and the bike popped in gear—first gear, just as planned.

When it's right, it's right. From the moment I began accelerating, I knew we were on our way. The bike handled effortlessly as I pointed her down the center of the strip. 90, 100, 110 mph, all while still in first gear. One thing that became immediately apparent to me was how loud the thing was. We're talking LOUD. I guess not having the steel tubular chassis of the old bike to help dampen some of the sound vibration was part of the tradeoff. I think my ears are still ringing as I write this.

120, 130, still climbing. A salt tail slings from the rear tire as we pick up speed. At this point I'm pretty confident in the way things are going. I glance at the tachometer on occasion, making sure I'm keeping it between 6,000 and 7,000 rpm. I have to back out of the throttle a little to keep her from over-revving, but that's to be expected. As I stare out of the tinted Plexiglas windshield, I'm impressed at how good visibility is. I begin my search for the 4-mile marker.

Somewhere between an eighth to a quarter of a mile from the 4, something unexpected happens. The bike begins to fishtail uncontrollably. I react immediately by deploying the high-speed parachute in hopes of straightening her back out. I also immediately follow up with the main chute, my thinking being that the high-speed chute will probably not be enough since I am now traveling somewhere in the neighborhood of 135–155 mph. I've given up on looking at the MoTeC display as other more pressing issues are at hand. Again, since the high-speed parachute is designed to brake at speeds of 250 mph or greater, at this point it's like kissing your sister. It doesn't really count.

A split second later the rear wheel locks up completely, and at this point I realize I'm going down. This is one of the worst feelings in the world, knowing you are about to crash and feeling so helpless because there's not a damn thing you can do about it. I at least have the confidence in knowing I did all the right things and didn't panic under pressure. As the bike went sideways into its initial fishtail, I did have the presence of mind to throw out the laundry.

Even in the event of a crash, you want the parachutes out to minimize the risk of injury to the driver and damage to the machine. We do utilize a mercury switch, which should automatically deploy the main chute if the bike is on its side, but my reason for deploying it manually was to regain control and try to avoid crashing altogether. For the second time, we would later find, the main bagged parachute only came part way out of its canister and never opened. I can't say whether it would have been enough to keep me from crashing, but it would have at least slowed the bike down considerably as it tumbled and slid on its side down the salt for nearly a quarter-mile.

When the rear wheel locked, the bike slid out from under me and slammed on its right side, skipping and bouncing at first, and then sliding uncontrollably for what felt like an eternity. I remember my biggest concern being that it didn't catch and pencil roll, which would have probably destroyed the machine, and all of its contents— of which I was a part. As it was, I remember once again looking out the side window as the salt was grinding by, lifting my head and trying to put as much distance as possible between me and the thin, Plexiglas window, the only thing separating me from the harsh outer environment. At one point it felt as though the bike might tumble completely over. I could actually see the salt skidding by at the top of the side windshield, meaning the bike was skidding momentarily in a slightly inverted position. We have a tiny lipstick camera mounted on the very tip of the tail which was actually ripped off during the slide, proof that at one point the bike was nearly upside down.

Luck was on our side as the remainder of the slide home went without incident. From start to finish (of the crash) the bike bounced and slid for nearly a quarter-mile. When it came to rest, I immediately radioed that I was okay. In my next breath I also told Denis that something broke, which caused the crash. It was kind of like my kid when caught doing something wrong: It wasn't my fault . . .

The crew was there in a matter of seconds. I waited calmly for help, unhurt but unhappy, too. Our test had come to a premature end. We would later learn that the motor lost oil pressure and seized all four rod bearings. This caused the rear wheel to lock up, which in turn spit me on the ground. It could have been much worse. As it was, I escaped without injury and the bike remained intact with only minimal damage to the body and side glass. As for the motor, well, two out of three ain't bad . . .

* * *

On another note: In the off-season before coming to Bonneville to run the new machine we lost a dear friend and a former member of our crew. Vern Brown passed away, leaving behind his lovely wife, Kip, and their children. He usually drove the tow vehicle for me and was always there to lend a hand. He was a class act and is missed dearly.

I have to tell you of a fond memory we all have of Vern on one of those restless nights before a speed trial. Somewhere in the wee hours of the night Vern got up to relieve himself in his hotel room and opened the door to the bathroom and stepped sleepily inside. The door closed behind him and before he could get a grasp of the situation at hand, he realized he had unknowingly stepped into the hallway of the Stateline Hotel (which is now the Nugget) and was stranded outside his room clad in white "bunhuggers" with little more than an embarrassed look on his face to hide behind.

As usual, the Stateline is a busy hotel and Mr. Brown wasn't alone in the hallway, as two elderly women passed nervously by and quickly disappeared into their room. He walked the hallway in search of Mr. Manning's room, where he proceeded to pound on the door until Denis allowed the half-naked intruder to enter. "I locked myself out of my room. Mind if I use your phone to call the front desk?" The two exchanged glances, comparing BVDs and Fruit of the Looms.

"Hello, my name is Vern Brown," his normally golden tone carrying a hint of embarrassment. "It appears I've locked myself out of my room. Could you be so kind as to send someone up with a key so I can get back inside? Oh yeah, and if a couple of elderly ladies reported a wild man walking the hallways in his underwear, that would be me. I assure you I'm harmless. I mistakenly stepped into the hallway while thinking I'd entered the latrine."

Such is life. We all miss you, Vern.

Chapter Fourteen
It's the Little Things

On Wednesday, July 28, we returned to the salt for our final test before our record attempt in September. We arrived in the afternoon to temperatures hovering around 100 degrees. The guys had arrived Monday, and were nearing completion of preparing an 8 1/2-mile course. Overall it looked really good, although it was a little wet due to rains earlier in the week.

Thursday morning we arrived ready for business. We did a quick dead engine tow test to make sure the bike was balanced and aligned properly, which it was, then prepared for our first motorized pass. The goal of this trip was to test several things, but of main concern

It's all about the toys... *Photo courtesy of Tricia Robinson*

were the parachutes (which at this point weren't working as well as we'd hoped), the transmission, and the handling of the bike at speed.

New rods, a new crank, and whole lot of money were injected into the motor to ensure it was ready for this week's session. There was no time for dyno testing, but we did fire the beast at home a couple of times and it sounded sweet. On a first gear shakedown run we ran into a little glitch that needed looking into. At a few clicks shy of 150 mph, I hit the high-speed chute release and both the high-speed and the backup chute deployed. From the cockpit, I have no way of knowing this has happened, and I assume everything is normal. The pull isn't any stronger than when just the high-speed is out, so everything *feels* normal. Of course, at only 150 mph, this isn't anything to write home about.

I then hit the main chute to see if the larger pilot chute we installed will pull the main bagged chute out properly. On the last trip, the bag kept hanging up in the tail section, never fully releasing or functioning properly. This time the bag pulled completely free of the bodywork into the outside air. The bag is pulled only partway from the chute, but not enough to allow it to open and help with the stopping process.

Just like in your car, I put my foot on the brake and slow *Big Red* to a stop. It takes a while, but then again this is a 1,500-pound motorcycle.

We examine the chutes and learn many things. The first is that the only bag that worked properly was the high-speed chute bag. The other two failed, but at least now we know why. As the lanyard tightened and was supposed to pull the bag from the chute, the lanyards tore from the bag on both the main chute and the back-up chute after only partial deployment. The bags were toast and would have to be replaced.

The good news was we had spares, but they were of a different design and were our second choice for a reason. The first bags were made of a durable, light canvas material. The lanyards themselves ripped, not the bags. The lanyards were made of a heavy draw-string material—obviously not heavy-duty enough. The backup bags were much lighter, made from fabric used on your favorite windbreaker—very light and probably very delicate. The lanyards on these just happened to be made from a heavier strap rather than string, our only saving grace. We repacked the chutes into the new bags (which, for some reason, were smaller); it was like trying to stuff 10 pounds of shit into a 5-pound bag. The bags were installed and the wedges put back in place.

The second pass was better, 185 mph and a clean shift into sec-ond gear. John's "attaboy" was almost in sight. (For a complete "attaboy," we needed to go through the entire range, first through fourth gear, cleanly.) When I hit the high-speed chute release, again both the high-speed and backup chutes came out together. This time the bag released the big chute just as it was supposed to and it opened perfectly, slowing me from 185 to about 90 in a matter of seconds. If I had only intended for this bad boy to come out it would have been a successful test. Had this happened at 300-plus mph, the big chute could literally rip the bike in half or at least cause a loss of control and an unsafe situation.

Aside from that, another pet peeve of mine is the foam wedges in the tail section. They have to jettison out, along with the pilot chute to begin the deployment process. Still in the development stage, these wedges are secured in place with masking tape. When the air ram hammers against the inside surface of the wedge, the tape is supposed to shear in half and the wedge goes flying into space, giving free passage to the parachutes. Sometimes they work, and sometimes they don't. The tape is borderline too strong, and about one in every three times I hit the button, the wedges make a "thud" sound as the ram hammers against them, but they don't move.

As technology advances, Denis came up with the sophisticated method of perforating the tape. Three holes wasn't enough, we found, but five . . . that was the magic number. They seemed to deploy more consistently with the masking tape perforated with five holes in each strip. I wonder if this technology was used on the space shuttle their first time testing parachutes. I'm certain NASCAR uses it . . .

On one pass, the top wedge actually fell out on its own. Luckily one of the crew members noticed it and radioed me of the situation, which allowed me to abort the run before anything tragic happened. More attention to this area would be needed when we returned home.

After a couple of near 200-mph runs, we noticed a severe vibration that wouldn't go away. It only happened at speed, but was bad enough to force me to back out of the throttle every time. On my final attempt, a side wind caught me off guard after releasing the main chute, pulling me instantly to the left side of the course and heading directly for a big red course marker. Try as I might, it was like a magnet, and there was an immediate attraction. The last 20 feet I actually locked up the rear wheel and skidded to a stop less than 2 feet to the right side of it. The skids were less than 2 inches from the edge of the course, and the bodywork was nearly resting against the PVC-framed marker.

But I didn't hit it.

A small victory, bordering on "attaboy" status. We were done. The vibration was too severe to continue without causing damage to the machine. We took her home and took her apart.

Many things were found that contributed to the vibration.

First of all, the front wheel was out of balance by more than 1 1/2 ounces. At 200 mph, that 1 1/2 ounces is magnified to nearly 60 pounds! The tire was also showing signs of trauma, as a deep crack became visible in its rubber carcass. Denis removed the tire and ran it through a band saw to examine it more closely. At several hundred dollars a lick, you don't want to do this too often.

The wheel was also examined and found to be out of true. There must have been significant forces working against us because it all looked perfect the last time we checked. Maybe it was excessive down-force pushing against the front end at speed. Maybe we hit something on the track. Or maybe crashing at 150 mph in the last test session a few weeks earlier boogered it. The latter made the most sense to me.

We also found the rear tire to be slightly out of balance. These were all things that could be fixed and improved upon. John also began work on a new wedge design that would be made of carbon fiber instead of our foam throwaway models held in with tape. The boys were on the right track.

About the time we decided to throw in the towel, an old-time military fighter came by just off the deck and scared the hell out everybody. Well, except for me, cause I knew we weren't being attacked—it was just my brother doing a very low flyby. My best friend Scott Jensen was flying copilot in the rear seat, still recovering from a recent motorcycle accident where he broke a number of ribs and his nose-picking finger. (He's a motorcycle cop and was in pursuit when a girl on a cell phone pulled out in front of him from a convenience store parking lot—ouch!) They were running a little late and managed to miss the entire show.

Down the way from us, BMW had set up camp on the salt and was preparing for a photo shoot for their magazine. They had next year's sports car there and had hired a professional driver to throw it around on the salt and get some cool pics. It had a carbon fiber boom on the right front corner with a camera attached to the end some eight feet away. He would drive around throwing the car sideways with salt spraying everywhere while filming himself from the extended boom. A second person would ride in the back seat on the left side to compensate for the additional weight of the camera and the boom, and would also operate a hand-held remote which controlled the camera. Pretty trick . . .

Anyway, they noticed my brother and Scott doing barrel rolls and dives in his antique fighter and decide to pay him a visit. The plane is a Nanchang, a Chinese trainer which is actually their version of a Russian Yak. It's all original and looks straight out of an old war movie.

Shortly after hanging with the race crew, my brother and Tricia—who replaced Scott as copilot and is normally a white-knuckled flier, took off in search of fame and fortune via the boys at BMW. Buddy (my brother) couldn't resist doing a couple of rolls and death-defying dives during their short flight to the other end of the salt. I thought Tricia would be puking, but when she got out she had this big shit-eating grin on her face. She was a born again flyer! After landing they were immediately surrounded by German cameramen and crewmembers involved in the photo shoot. They set up shop around my brother's plane and started clicking off pictures.

That was the easy part.

They then wanted to get some action pictures with the car and the plane humming down the salt side by side. They ask my brother what is the slowest speed at which he could safely fly beside the car at just above ground level. Moments later you see this tiny blue-gray sports car ripping down the salt at 110 mph with this army-green military fighter only a few feet back and to the left, perfectly centered in the viewfinder of the camera's eye which is carving through the wind still attached to the right front corner of the car! What an amazing shot.

When the shooting was all over the producer asked if my brother wouldn't mind taking him for a ride. So naturally he did what any red-blooded ex-motorcycle racer would do and started showboating with his new captive audience. A few barrel rolls and low flybys later the German producer was still smiling but looked a little green around the edges.

* * *

The Southern California Timing Association (SCTA) ran their regularly scheduled August meet at Bonneville while we were at home mending our wounds. There were a couple of notable runs. Jimmy Odom, in the twin-engine Suzuki Hyabusa streamliner *Ack Attack* made a respectable debut, having passed his low speed tests at 150, 180, and 200 mph without a hitch. He then turned around and made a good clean run at a little over 220 mph. A new contender had thrown his hat in the ring.

But the big news was Sam Wheeler.

Sam Wheeler has been racing and fine-tuning his Kawasaki-powered *E-Z-Hook* streamliner for the better part of 12 years. On August 18, 2004, Sam made a one-way pass of 330 mph. On August 19, he made a return run of 334 mph, for a 332 average . . . a new world record! (Technically an SCTA and Bonneville Nationals, Inc. (BNI) record, only because the Fédération Internationale de Motocyclisme (FIM) sanctioning body wasn't around to witness the feat.)

No matter the technicalities, Sam Wheeler is the man. Dave Campos is a class act and at this point has held the record for over 15 years. He is a great ambassador to the sport and is still officially the world record holder, but even he recognized Sam's accomplishment. Once again, the bar had been raised.

Chapter Fifteen
International Motorcycle Speed Trials by BUB

M onday, September 6, 2004. We arrive at the salt and proceeded to the pit area. At noon there is still over an eighth-
inch of standing water in the pit area. The First Annual BUB Bash,
a week of racing sponsored by BUB Enterprises, was off to a shaky
start. We took a ride down the course in my rented mini van—the
soccer mom special—and found it equally wet, especially in the

Sam Wheeler was all smiles before his run. He won $10,000 at this event for
achieving the top time of the meet, with a top speed through the lights averaging
322 mph. *Photo courtesy of Meggan Bechtol*

measured mile, which ran from the 4- to the 5-mile markers. It was a full 10-mile course.

This event is rather unique, in that there is approximately $50,000 in prize money: $10,000 for top time of the meet (which one of the three streamliners entered was sure to take), $10,000 for the top conventional bike, $5,000 for top American V-twin, $5,000 for top metric twin, and on down the line. There was also a $5,000 award for the top speed per cubic centimeters, meaning a 50-cc machine going 100 mph would take home the bacon over a 1,000-cc machine that went 200 mph. This would turn out to be one of the more interesting classes of competition.

This was our first attempt at promoting a major all-motorcycle event of this magnitude. The money ensured the top dogs would all be there. The press came in droves, as did an impressive number of spectators. We had to separate the race team from the track staff, both of which were either already BUB crewmembers or BUB employees, which proved to be disastrous at times. A BUB family member was basically left in charge to run things on the event side, which didn't sit well with many. A few recruits also joined in the mayhem, but all in all, the event did what we set out to do;—to bring recognition and a sense of reward to those who put it on the line for the sake of two-wheeled land speed racing.

My hat is off to our race crew, who worked tirelessly to layout and mark the course, as well as to prepare the most awesome streamliner to grace the salt. These guys are my heroes. The event staff was a little green, but they put in a good first effort and went home knowing what it would take to improve next year's event.

My hat's off to Ken Draper for coordinating between the long and short course runs and keeping things orderly and safe. Larry Coleman did an excellent job announcing. His many years of involvement in the motorcycle industry shone through, with his knowledgeable commentary and entertaining stories. Ken Cooper and his crew manned the tech inspection area (which was oddly labeled "scrutineering") and did an excellent job. There were many others involved, and we couldn't have pulled it off without them. A big "thank you" goes out to all of them.

Due to the wet conditions, no one ran the first day. On Tuesday, things began looking up. In just one day the entire pit area had dried. The standing water was gone. I took a ride in our rented mini-van down the course to see if the measured mile was also dry. Jimmy Odom rode along with me, equally concerned. For those of you who don't know, Jimmy is a legend in his own right. In his day, he was one of the toughest competitors in Class C racing. He raced against many of the greats of the time, including Gary Scott, Gene Romero, Kenny Roberts, Jim Rice and all the other top dogs. I remember as a kid going to watch these guys duke it out on the mile and 1/2-mile ovals. Jimmy wore the number 18 on his bike and rode with an aggressive, caution-to-the-wind style.

And now here he was, cruising with me in the van, sharing his thoughts and concerns about course conditions and sharing old racing stories.

There were still puddles on the course—mainly in the measured mile, the fastest part of the track. Anywhere else it might have been okay to run, but the center of the course is where it counts, and for us, hitting standing water at or near 300 mph wasn't an option. We decided to wait a little longer and see if it would improve.

The crew went about preparing my bike and, as happens all too often, we ran into our first little problem. After the cheesy setup we used at our last test session, where the rear wedges that conceal the parachutes were held in with perforated masking tape, the new plan was to redesign the wedges out of carbon fiber instead of foam and come up with a better way of attaching them to the body. I never liked the foam wedges from the start. The bike is so trick, and these just seemed like an oversight, like something thrown in there at the last minute just to get the job done.

Well, the carbon fiber idea got canned. The new plan was to make the wedges out of denser foam, and to attach them to the bike using shear pins. There would be four in each wedge, one on either side at the top and on the bottom. There were little aluminum inserts in the bodywork where the pins would go through into an insert in the wedge itself. When I hit the release button, an air cylinder would slam against the backside of the wedge, breaking the shear pins in two, and sending the wedge and the pilot chute into space. We tried this new design at home several times and it worked every time.

At Bonneville, I hit the chute release and there was a loud thud, but the wedges didn't budge. "Crap," I thought. "Here we go again . . ."

There's just something about being out there that you can't explain. The Bonneville curse. Things you try over and over at home that never fail will almost certainly cause you grief when you're out on the great white plains. Luckily we were still in the pits when we tested the new wedge design just once more for good luck.

After a few expletives and unhappy thoughts, I brought John and Howard over to share my pain. As is their personality, rather than kicking the tires and coming up with a few nasty profanities of their own, they went to work on solving the problem. Howard had the bright idea of shortening the pads on the end of the rams that slammed against the wedges to force them out. This would increase the momentum of the ram before it hit the wedge, creating a greater impact. Okay, that made sense. John, meanwhile, removed the bottom two shear pins from each wedge, reducing the amount of force needed to knock the wedges from the body. There was hope yet.

"Okay. Hit the button," John commanded. I did and the wedge and the pilot chute went flying. John just scored another "attaboy."

We were now all dressed up with nowhere to go. Jimmy Odom and I took another cruise down the course and determined that it was still too wet to run. We would pack it in and return in the morning in hopes of dryer conditions and a chance to run.

The next morning we arrived early and watched the sunrise from the front seat of our van as we cruised the course at a fairly brisk pace. I was only concerned with the measured mile at this point, as the rest of it was good enough. There was no more standing water—or even puddles for that matter—but it was still wet as hell. The last quarter-mile or so refused to dry out. The regular bikes would probably get their chance to run today, but as for us and Jimmy, it was still pretty sketchy.

The press took advantage of our down time and invited themselves to the party. Fox TV asked if they could film a couple of segments live from our pits. These guys were for real. They had the hottie anchorwoman, the camera crew, and even some director type who just looked important. I did four separate segments, and when I was through, Denis moved in and parked it in front of them and threatened not to leave until they were completely out of film. Okay, so I'm exaggerating a *little* bit, but he talked about everything from carbon fiber to rent control. The guy is way too comfortable in front of an audience . . .

Sam Wheeler came rolling in about midmorning, his record-breaking *E-Z-Hook* streamliner in tow. This guy is too cool for words. He doesn't even bother to show up for the first couple of days, figuring all he needed was a couple of good runs to pocket the 10 grand and maybe leave with an international record to boot. If it were anybody else I'd think they were a little bit cocky—but not Sam. This guy is the real deal. Every run he makes now is at a record pace. He's had some 12-plus years to dial in his machine and that baby flat hauls ass. One day I am confident that we will beat him, but right now he's on top of his game. We'll have our turn.

Around midday, things get under way. Bikes begin to line up at both the short and long course entrance with the intent of burning up the salt. Right off, we notice conditions are a bit sketchy. Every bike passing through the timing lights experienced moderate amounts of wheelspin and seat cushion inhalation. The "pucker factor" was at an all time high. Pete Davis made it through unscathed, laying down a record pass with little problems. He was one of the few exceptions to the rules.

We decided to roll down to the end of the course and set up shop at the long course entrance. My original plan was to run hard until the 4-mile, then hit the high-speed chute and coast through the slop. This would at least give me a "feel" for how the measured mile was without hanging it all out on the first run.

When we arrived, one of the riders who had just completed a run on a modified V-Rod Harley told us it was scary as hell. He'd nearly lost control of his bike flying through the measured mile, the wet salt being too slippery and too soft in places to be considered safe. One by one, others braved the conditions and made their runs. A conventional bike is one thing, but a 24-foot long, two-wheeled guided missile is another. I'd been through standing water before at speed, and told myself I wouldn't make that mistake again.

I still wanted to make a pass, and suggested we run to the three and throw out the laundry. We could hit maybe 250 or better and at least have a shakedown run behind us. Denis considered the idea, but decided against it. He didn't want to put the bike or myself at risk in the event of a parachute failure. I didn't argue his decision, thinking it best to wait it out. At this point, Sam and Jimmy hadn't even considered running. We returned to the pits, saving our bullets and laying low.

Thursday, September 9, 2004. We were now beginning to run out of time. With only a day and half left to run (the meet was to end on Friday at noon), the pressure was starting to build. I found Sam Wheeler and asked if he'd like to ride along and view the course with me. Jimmy had yet to arrive, so we made the inspection without him.

The course was better, but still pretty wet where it counted. We stopped in the middle of the track to pick up a piece of debris. It turned out to be a bone fragment, I think possibly a hip joint because it was round and smooth. From what animal, I have no idea. Besides the wet conditions, we had the wind to deal with. From right to left, a constant breeze had developed and didn't seem to be leaving anytime soon.

Sam wasn't so sure about running, but I knew we would take the gamble. We were promoting the event. If we didn't run, how could we expect anyone else to—especially the streamliners. When we returned to the pits we packed our gear and motored to the end of the course to prepare for our first run.

The bone fragment turned out to be a bigger deal than we initially thought. Jeff Boyle saw it and said it was bad mojo and to get rid of it. Don Eslinger, a team member and good friend of mine decided to throw it in the trash—out of sight, out of mind.

You'd think that would be the end of it. Wrong.

Buzzy, also convinced the bone was jinxed, retrieved it from the trash can and went behind the trailer and did some sort of spiritual dance while chanting to the gods. He then tells me the bone I found is bad luck, but not to worry, he exorcised it and removed all the bad spirits. And, he tells me, if that still didn't work he tossed the bone into someone else's pit—Jimmy Odom's. And this is the guy I trust my life to, the guy who helps me pack my parachutes before each run. We had a good nervous laugh and forgot all about the evil piece of debris.

We were to make the first pass that day and, I have to admit, I was a little nervous about how the bike would react at speed going through the lights. I was staged under the race trailer's huge canopy out of the sun and the elements. As the tow vehicle pulled me away, I was immediately blinded by the sunlight as soon as I was clear of the canopy from the trailer. It was still pretty early and the sun was staring me straight in the face. I accelerated hard at first, but was admittedly having trouble staying focused with my limited vision. Then the wind kicked in and I remember crabbing over, the bike leaning hard right—into the wind. This was not good, but the bike ran great and shifted through all the gears flawlessly. At 237 mph I'd had enough and pulled the high-speed chute. I had aborted the run at about the 3-mile mark, and coasted to a stop just in front of the slop.

This was still the fastest pass of the meet on our new machine, and easily the fastest run down the salt so far. It had so much more potential, and I was a little disappointed in myself for not trying to tough it out and push a little harder. When it's right, it's right, and only then will we set the world on fire. I was confident in our equipment and our crew—and our capabilities—but Denis counts on me to make the right decisions every time we are out there. We packed our gear and headed back to the pits to gear up for our next run. The next hurdle was to break 250.

After seeing our shakedown pass, the competition decided if we could do it, so could they. Both Jimmy Odom (Suzuki-powered *Ack Attack* streamliner), and Sam Wheeler (Kawasaki-powered *E-Z-Hook*) staged at the far end of the course ready to do business. In the meantime several conventional bikes took their turn on the course, but it was evident that conditions were less than perfect. Wheelspin and gusting winds limited top speeds and dampened the spirits of many.

I waited at the pits to watch Jimmy run before joining my crew back at the staging area for Round Two. It seemed like forever, but after coming by and asking what it was like out there, he returned to his place at the front of the line and put the hammer down.

I have to tell you, Mike Akatiff's *Ack Attack* team and BUB do things in a very different manner. We take baby steps, testing and evaluating every step of the way. I am a test pilot, as is Jimmy. But he and his team owner, Mike Akatiff, seem to be operating on a much narrower time frame.

Right off, I see him hurling down the salt, a plume of white sailing in the air behind him. He is accelerating hard, and the rear tire is spinning furiously, traction seemingly lacking from the equation. Nonetheless, he makes an impressive run at 273 mph. Top time of the meet so far. Keep in mind that his fastest previous run was in the 220–225 neighborhood. While we were taking baby steps, Mr. Odom was seemingly glory bound in only his first season of land speed racing. I take my hat off to him and Mike for coming to speed so quickly, but I am also concerned about their approach. This is a dangerous sport, and carelessness can bite you in the ass when you least expect it.

Sam is next, but this time I am lined up behind him, watching from the staging area because we will be running shortly thereafter.

Sam plays the game exactly how it should be played. He has been doing this for a long time and knows his machine inside and out. He has fine-tuned it over the years and is now in contention to take away the crown. He is already the unofficial fastest man on two wheels. He is not the recognized world record holder because his fastest recorded runs were at a Southern California Timing Association (SCTA) club event, not an international event with the proper sanctioning bodies and international rules in play. All his hard work and years of testing and paying his dues have put him where he is today. Right now virtually every pass Sam makes is above the 300-mph mark, his most recent runs being above the world record mark of 322.

His motor fires and his crew send him on his way. I get goose bumps just watching. He disappears into a sea of white, his motor screaming at the top of its lungs. The turbocharger muffles the sound, but gives the extra boost needed for his tiny motor to get the job done. The announcer comes on the PA shortly after Sam comes to a stop at the far end of the course some 8–10 miles away. His speed: 322 and change! Sam is almost assured of the 10 grand for top time of the meet. He has also just completed half of the required two runs needed to become the official new record holder. Dave Campos, the current record holder, was there to witness the feat.

Sam decides against making a return run. He reasons that this run was to take Denis' money, and tomorrow will be for the record. There may be more to it than he was letting on, but you can't argue with success.

Our next run was a disaster. As soon as I tried to bring the skids up, while still behind the tow vehicle, the right skid remained partially deployed. I radioed the tow vehicle to confirm it was still out. I released from the tow vehicle and toggled the skids repeatedly. The damned thing wouldn't come in. Denis radioed me and told me to abort. What a pisser.

Rather than go all the way back to the pits, we remained at the staging end of the course and set up shop to work on the skid. Frustration and disappointment filled the air. Denis and John inspected the skid and made a few adjustments. It was still a bit lazy in retracting, but it did function. John voted that we operate the skid in question 10 times. If it fully retracted every time, we would return to the staging area and take up where we left off. We all counted together as Denis toggled the skids. Even though the right side skid was definitely slower than the left, it retracted fully every time.

In hindsight it was probably a good thing that the skid failed when it did. Jimmy had just run at 273 mph and Sam at 322. The adrenaline was at an all-time high. Our original plan was to top

250, but with Jimmy's run of 273, I probably would have tried to at least match or beat his mark. Probably not the smartest move, but perhaps within our grasp. Then Sam comes along and puts down a hot one. Damn.

My mom grabs Tricia's hand and tells her she's really nervous. Tricia knows we have a game plan, but also knows how competitive I am. 322 mph. Damn.

Then, with the aborted run, things seemed to simmer down a bit. Reason returned as testosterone and one-upsmanship became less of an issue. By the time we were ready to go, another hour had passed. This time the sun wasn't much of an issue. I accelerated hard and had good traction and plenty of power at my disposal. The side wind returned and once again I found myself crabbing into it, leaning dangerously askew. I kept my foot in it until 260 mph and hit the high-speed chute. I was only at the 3-mile at the time, but needed time to get back on course in the middle of the track.

Most people thought it odd that I accelerated through the measured mile with the small parachute trailing behind me but I wanted to see how the bike reacted under power through the slop. It didn't seem to be as big a problem as the wind. Once through, I deployed the main chute and was immediately yanked hard to the left. I nearly took out half of the left side course markers, somehow just missing them by mere inches. At 260 mph, we checked off another rung in our ladder to the top. Tomorrow we would try for 275 and then hopefully 300.

As nerve-racking as our day had been, it was about to get worse.

As the conventional bikes took their turn on the salt, Jimmy Odom and Mike Akatiff readied their machine for another run. To deal with the excessive wheelspin they experienced earlier, Mike installed a set of custom made "wings" that were intended to put additional down force on the rear tire. The only thing I know about wings is that they were originally designed to make things fly. With 10 grand on the line for top time, they figured if they could get the power to the ground they had a legit shot at the cash.

Again, I take my hat off to these guys for pushing as hard as they do. We all lined up beside the measured mile to watch his run. We knew he'd be fast, but weren't ready for what happened next.

Off in the distance the shiny silver bullet came into view. It looked really fast with far less salt spraying behind as on his earlier run. I looked just above the timing tower at the flagpole and noticed the American flag standing erect, blowing straight toward us. That meant there was a substantial side wind. That wasn't good.

As Jimmy came closer, it looked like he was really hauling ass. I mean, he looked as fast as Sam. The measured mile was coming into his view and I had my doubts as to how well he could maneuver through the slop. With the gusting winds and the heat of the day drawing additional moisture to the surface, conditions were far from favorable. I'd say the winds at the time he entered the lights were at least 5–7 mph coming from right to left. We normally run in 3 mph or less.

The one problem with land speed racing is that in order to have a flat place several miles long to run, there will be wind issues. In Jimmy and Mike's defense, even if you are monitoring the wind, it can change at any stage of the run. Even if it's calm across the whole salt flat, that can all change the moment you take off. There are no guarantees. You give it your best shot and hope it goes your way. I know this firsthand, having been blown off course and having many close calls of my own.

Entering the measured mile, the *Ack Attack* streamliner was in trouble. You could hear Jimmy back out of the throttle—maybe due to the wind, maybe due to the wet, slippery conditions. He was going so fast that just coasting through the lights would be quite an achievement. But that's not how Jimmy Odom operates.

This guy is in the Motorcycle Hall of Fame for a reason. He knows about pushing the limits. He knows no matter how good the machine, it takes an even better pilot to get the most out of it and make things happen. His team is built around that philosophy.

Just into the measured mile, we heard the motor start to rev again, and rev hard. Jimmy had just grabbed a handful of throttle and was going to attempt to muscle his way through the wind and soft, slippery, rutted salt. A plume of white emerges from behind as the bike begins to drift sideways. He is leaning hard right into the wind and on the gas. It was a bold move, but one that I'm sure if he had time to reconsider, he might have tried a different strategy.

Or maybe not.

In the next instant the rear of the bike starts to pass the front, and the front end lifts into the air. He tries to correct, but with the front wheel no longer on the ground he has no means of control and is left helpless, unable to do anything but (hopefully) survive. The "oohs" and "aahs" sounded off as my mom screamed and Tricia covered her face in fear. Jimmy tumbled out of control somewhere near 300 mph, taking out the timing lights and a course marker in the process. As the bike rolled, the canopy snapped off, leaving him exposed and vulnerable. Through all of this, he was still going very fast. His emergency parachute deployed and luckily quickly brought him to a stop. Seconds later he was out of the bike and on his feet unharmed.

A collective sigh of relief echoed from the sidelines. The fact that he was able to walk away from this horrific crash is a true testament to the fine craftsmanship and attention to detail the designers and builders of these machines have reached. Luck was also on his side.

The wings that helped give additional traction were both peeled from the machine in the crash. I still believe that wings were meant to fly, and that's what the *Ack Attack* streamliner did. When the bike was level and the wings equal length from the ground, I'm sure they were a benefit for giving the extra traction they were looking for. But as the bike leaned, one wing was now higher in the air, the other closer to the ground, and now they were both having a much different effect than was originally intended. This is where additional testing might have come in handy.

As they were picking the pieces of the wounded streamliner from the course, Denis wrapped his arms around Tricia and tried to comfort her. "This is why we take baby steps, sweetheart," his grip remained constant until her shaking subsided. My mom had seen it all before and was already pretty thick-skinned about racing; Tricia was paying her dues . . .

Chapter Sixteen
Dodging the Bullet

D enis always spoke of us returning to Australia to take care of unfinished business. We already owned the fastest one-way pass on a motorcycle, but with the world record seemingly within reach, he wanted to return in March 2005 and make it official.

Not all of us on the crew shared his belief that we were ready. Sure, the new bike was more than a capable contender, but it was too soon. We still needed more testing to be fully prepared to take on the world. Deep down I think Denis believed this as well, but he was never one to miss opportunity, and his forward thinking and eternal optimism kept everyone on their feet.

A vintage Indian racer. *Photo courtesy of Nathan Allred, Treasure Photography*

A meeting was scheduled among key members of the team. We had two more tentative dates left on the calendar in which we could run at Bonneville. The first week of October or the last week of the same month. We decided that we needed to reach the 300 mark here, if we were to pack our bags and head abroad. The official record still stood at 322, which was still a ways away. A 300-mph showing and four months of preparation made the most sense. (It would take a full month for the bike to reach the shores of Australia by boat.) That would give us time for more engine development—more horsepower is always a good thing—and a chance to readdress the parachute deployment system (those damn wedges), among other things.

There are benefits and disadvantages to a machine as complex as ours. To stay on top of every little thing is almost impossible for any one person to do. It takes a level of devotion and compulsiveness that not many can deliver. John and Denis both spend countless hours trying to stay on top of it, but they both have businesses to run that also demand a great deal of their time and energy. Unlike the big factory efforts involved in say, Grand Prix racing, where racing is their only business and there are no outside distractions, our efforts rely on those who hold down full-time jobs unrelated to our sport. After putting in countless hours on the job during the day, they come to the race shop and work into the wee hours of the night for no pay and little recognition. These guys are my heroes, but even heroes can have a bad day.

* * *

Due to the changing weather, it was decided that we would return to Bonneville to run at the beginning of October. The goal would be 300 mph. If we reached it, Australia would be next. I felt the added pressure on my shoulders not to let the team down. I was determined to do my part and was prepared to pull out all the stops and squeeze every ounce of speed out of *Big Red* to obtain our goal. It wasn't going to be because of me if we weren't able to make the trek across the pond.

Pete Davis, Buzzy, Bobo, and Kevin Kondra left with Denis on September 28 for Bonneville to cut in the course and put up the markers. When they got there, the salt was hard and dry. Pete and Denis hooked up the drags and began grooming the salt while Bobo, Buzzy, and Kevin went about the unenviable task of drilling the salt and standing up the course markers. Since we would be running on the same course that we used for the BUB Speed Trials, the boys were lucky to find the holes still existed from the previous event and just needed to be cleaned so the markers could be inserted.

Where they weren't so lucky was the fact that Denis, our fear-less leader, decided it best to start dragging from the side of the course and managed to fill in a good portion of the holes with fresh salt from the heavy drag he was towing behind his rig. Thanks, BUB!

And then there was that damn bone. The round hip bone with the bad mojo from the last meet, that may or may not have contributed to Jimmy Odom's spectacular crash, showed up again. Buzzy took it upon himself to do the right thing and place it under quarantine this time. He moved it far away from our pit and the course and sprayed a bright orange circle of paint around it, which he later told us was to contain the evil spirits. He wasn't taking any chances with the possessed skeletal demon this time. Hmmm.

After all their hard work, they returned to the hotel for the evening, only to be met shortly after by a thundering downpour of rain. Maybe it was the bone calling the gods to come to its defense, or maybe it was Mother Nature. You decide.

The next morning, Thursday, the rest of us were to leave home for the salt. We were packed and ready to head out the door when the phone rang. Denis told everyone to stay put until he examined the course. It rained all night and things didn't look good. He was heading out and would call back within the hour. Not good . . .

The return phone call finally came with Denis standing at the 9-mile, his voice optimistic and with good reason. The course was wet, but not overly wet. They figured they could save it and that we should get it in gear and hit the road. There was still a 30 percent chance of rain that day, but it wasn't raining then, and the official word was we were going to run. That was all we needed to hear.

Some seven-plus hours later we arrived on the salt to have our first look. It was six in the afternoon Utah time. It had rained on us for 60 of the last 80 miles traveled, but for some reason, the rain decided to take up residence atop the last mountain range just before Wendover. It looked ugly, but as long as it didn't cross the state line, we were in business.

We met with Denis and the crew and viewed their handiwork. The course looked amazing. It was way smoother than the last time I was out, and pretty darn dry. By morning I was convinced it would be perfect. The measured mile, which looked so ugly during the BUB Speed Trials, was in perfect shape—just looking at it made you want to go fast. I was excited and felt confident we could do business here.

October 1. We arrived on the salt around 8:30. We were running a little late because of a little mishap back at the hotel. (Someone left the lights on in our car and killed the battery, so we needed a jump. Since I was driving, I guess that someone must have been me.) When we got there the bike was already out and on its stand. The crew was busying themselves with various tasks, which included final course preparation and last-minute adjustments to the bike.

Just before we were ready to make our first attempt, I asked if we could fire off the wedges one time just to ease my mind that they were functioning properly. Denis and John agreed, so I wrapped my hand around the right hand control stick and hit the deployment button on the high-speed chute.

A soft "thud" was heard, but the wedge didn't budge. My heart sank into my chest a little deeper as the thought of going extremely fast and not being able to stop crossed my mind. We decided to try the main chute and the same "thud" and the same disappointment ensued. Neither wedge budged. *Here we go again,* I thought.

John had glued new inserts into the wedges that the shear pins would be pressed into. He also reinforced the section of the wedges where the ram made contact, and these reinforcements altered the shape somewhat. We thought we had a good fit, but it was obvious they were still too tight. After sanding and massaging the wedges into submission, we tested them again and this time they both worked perfectly.

The bike was set on the ground and the rest of the crew had taken their position at various locations down the course. We were about to fire the bike when Denis and John stopped the countdown procedure because they were both unsure about something under the side panel of the outer shell. I didn't know what it was, as I was already strapped inside waiting the signal to light the fire and get under way. It's a little unnerving knowing you are about to put your life on the line and wondering if everything's okay with your equipment. The parachute wedges are already a pet peeve of mine, but having the crew second-guessing themselves right before the final seconds of a run tends to put a strain on one's confidence.

In their defense, I'd gladly wait another 15 minutes while they confirmed or denied there was a problem rather than being sent on my way while they scratched their heads and crossed their fingers.

Finally, I got the go ahead and the motor was lit. I took a deep breath and tried to put any unhappy thoughts behind me. The bike ran well and I got off to a good start. As I crossed the levee break at around the 2-mile marker, I felt a fairly strong side wind, which had me leaning to the right and drifting left. As I continued to pick up speed, things only got worse. I lifted from the throttle and had my doubts as to whether or not to finish the run.

No sooner had the wind rained on my parade than it was gone. I quickly mashed the pedal and pointed *Big Red* toward the center of the course. I pulled the high-speed release at the 4 and rolled out of the throttle at 280 mph—not bad for our first attempt off the trailer. As I coasted down to a reasonable speed at which to deploy the larger main parachute, something unexpected happened . . . it came out on its own, without me actually ever touching the button. I was about to deploy it anyway, so there was no major drama. But it would have been nice if I was the one controlling what was happening, which apparently wasn't the case.

All in all, the crew was happy with our first run. I told Denis about the problem with the wedge releasing prematurely, which he acknowledged, but still didn't seem overly concerned about. I dragged John and Buzzy into the picture along with Pete. Together we fit a new set of wedges to the machine and taped off all air cavities in front of the parachute chambers, hoping that air pressure building at speed might have been the culprit and this was the fix. At this point my confidence in the damned thing was severely in doubt.

We had a little downtime as the midday sun brought along an annoying breeze that wouldn't go away. It varied from 2 to 5 mph, sometimes a little greater—too much to run in in any case. We decided to wait until later in the afternoon when the sun was beginning to dip. Like water-skiing, the conditions are usually best shortly after sunup and shortly before sundown. Unlike water-skiing, however, there was a severe lack of bikini-clad women anywhere to be found.

Several miles down the salt, a film crew was busy preparing a set for an upcoming movie, *The World's Fastest Indian*, starring Anthony Hopkins who would be portraying Burt Munro, a famous speed-racer from New Zealand. A few of us ventured onto their set and marveled at their re-creation of a Bonneville Speed Trial in the early 1960s. Everything from an original scoring tower to 10-cent hot dogs and Burma Shave ads made you feel like you were stepping into another time zone.

I met with one of the stagehands named Lucas who filled us in a little about their project. Burt Munro was a talented builder, innovator, and racer. He held a record for the fastest sidecar in New Zealand which was only recently broken. He'd raced the Isle of Man TT, as well as many other world class events, before crating up his hand-built Indian-powered streamliner and shipping it across the pond to compete at the world famous Bonneville Salt Flats, where he set several records. Pretty cool stuff.

Back in the twenty-first century and our own Bonneville adventure, it was now late in the day and the wind was still a bit iffy at best. A herd of four-wheelers gathered around our pit hoping to see a show but were told we would only run if the wind died down soon. They didn't stay long, but were impressed just the same after getting to check out our long, red steed. Their quads topped out somewhere around 40 mph and after hearing of our plans to go 300, they had a new respect for their two-wheeled cousins.

At around six in the evening it became evident that we were running out of time. The wind was still buffeting, but our money was on the calm before darkness. Denis sent the crew down the salt to various positions with wind meters in hand. John strapped me into the bike while Don read off the checklist. With everything ready, we sat and waited while, one by one, reports filtered in that the wind was, in fact, subsiding. With a picture perfect sunset at our backs, the motor roared to life and howled into the fiery orange sky. It was dusk, and it was now or never. After one last check down course, Denis gave me the go-ahead, and the tow vehicle reeled in the slack.

Moments later I was accelerating hard down the middle of the course. It was a little eerie running this late in the day with the sun at my back and every nook and cranny in the salt highlighted by the tiniest of shadows. As I approached the levee break, the wind seemed to lay dormant, permitting entry without much of a challenge. I watched as the speedometer danced in ever increasing increments, the tach running close to redline as each shift pushed me harder into the back of my seat pan.

The bike was working great, the motor was screaming, and the tires were gripping surprisingly well. It started out as one of those runs where everything just seemed to click, our goal seemingly in reach.

Just when I thought we were finally going to join the elusive 300-mph club, all hell broke loose. As I entered the fourth mile, the onboard fire extinguishing system deployed unexpectedly, filling my cockpit with a sudsy cocktail of fire retardant and water! The best way I can describe it is like going through the automatic car wash with the windows open. When the heavy stream of soapy, foaming water coated my windshield, it was lights out. Add to that the fact that it was also spraying all over me, the nozzle focusing a fair amount of its energy directly onto the shield of my helmet. All the while I was building speed, and at this point traveling at 290 mph. Blind.

I'd never felt so alone and helpless in all my life. For a brief moment I was piloting this thing in total darkness, my only thoughts were that I couldn't panic—going way too fast for that. Keep it pointed straight, or what I think is straight, and hope for the best. I carefully took my left hand off the control stick and raised my shield, hoping to get a better view. Instead I got a face full of the foamy cocktail my shield was apparently keeping at bay. I tilted my head forward and let the shield deflect the spray while trying to look out from underneath. Pardon my French, but that was one scary son of a bitch.

As bad as that was, things were about to get worse.

Like in the carwash, the suds eventually subsided. As a distorted but somewhat clearer image of the salt and horizon returned, I realized

I'd become disoriented as to how far I'd traveled down the course. I immediately hit the high-speed chute, which worked nicely as planned. Because I had no idea whether I had 3 miles or 300 feet left to get her stopped, I then tripped the main chute release, my only thoughts being that I wanted this nightmare to be over. The whole time, this dripping foamy crap was everywhere, reminding me that sometimes things can go terribly wrong when you least expect them.

Important things, like the main parachute failing to come out when it's supposed to.

I couldn't believe it. That damned wedge stayed put once again, concealing the parachute and limiting my chances of stopping safely once again. As I barreled down the salt, coasting at somewhere around 260, I began to have my doubts as to having enough room to get stopped before I run out of salt. At the end of the course is another levee. My final option was to maneuver to my left and hopefully get her stopped in the loose, soft, crusty layers of ungroomed salt—not necessarily upright, but at least not head first into the levee wall, which I'm sure would hurt more. Grrrrrr.

I started applying the rear brake, which is in no way intended for use anywhere above, say 100 mph, and even then it is the main parachute that is supposed to do most of the work. It seemed to work initially, but quickly faded away and left me wondering what could possibly go wrong next.

Howard was pretty far down course and saw what was happening and radioed to me that the main chute wasn't out but everything looked fine. I responded in a rather heated voice that I was not fine, had no parachutes, and now no brakes. He looked ahead and reassured me I still had a couple of miles left. That was the single smartest thing anyone could have done for me at the time. I was pretty disoriented and had no clue where I was on the salt. Just knowing I still had enough room to get her stopped safely was comforting beyond words.

I kept reapplying the brakes, and from time to time they would actually slow me down considerably. The slower I got, the better they began to work. Just before I came to a stop I radioed Howard and told him to get me out of this thing immediately. By now he was blazing down the salt beside me in his rent-a-car, matching my pace, and keeping me in his sights. When I stopped, smoke billowed from behind. *Big Red* was on fire.

Howard approached the burning machine, not sure what to expect and concerned for his own safety. He wasn't wearing any fire protective clothing and was risking his own neck by even getting near me. I remembered him trying unsuccessfully to dislodge the canopy. I reached up from inside and grabbed the inner release and popped it loose. He tossed it aside while I undid my harness and cool suit. I was never so happy to see him. "Get me out," was all I could say.

It only took a matter of seconds for Howard to pull me from the machine and free me from danger. The medics immediately gathered around to see if I was okay. This all happened in a matter of seconds. Then, just like in the movies, a huge explosion echoed across the salt and our beautiful machine burst at the seams. The rear tire exploded unexpectedly, taking huge chunks of carbon fiber body parts and sending them into the air in all directions. The glowing red brake rotor and boiling fluid in the toasted calipers put off more heat than the Mickey Thompson LSR tire could bear. Smoke was now pouring from inside as Buzzy, the only crewmember wearing a fire retardant suit, emptied a couple of extinguishers into the burning streamliner. Unfortunately for the entire crew, it's too little, too late. The damage was already done.

Luckily, I walked away unharmed, but for the time being, *Big Red* was dead.

Part Three
Opportunity of a Lifetime

Chapter Seventeen
A Change for the Better

Another frustrating season came to an end. At times I questioned if we really had what it takes. Seeing the *Ack Attack* streamliner going so fast right from the get-go made me wonder. The following season was a disaster in many ways. Too much rain made the salt soft and bumpy. We opted not to run and instead focus on rebuilding our machine.

Altogether, 2005 was a year I'd rather forget.

Besides not being able to run, our business was having growing pains. We were losing money at an enormous rate. One day, in an act of desperation, Denis went on a firing spree and let several

A cool shot of the *Ack Attack*—my new ride. *Photo courtesy of Nathan Allred, Treasure Photography*

of his key people go. I was one of them. BUB Enterprises was slowly becoming a family-owned and operated affair. It never sat well with his son or daughter-in-law that I was his right-hand man in the company. I planned on retiring there, and now I was unemployed and, consequently, no longer a member of the racing team.

I was bitter about his decision—I helped make Manning a rich man, but also knew life goes on and other opportunities would eventually present themselves, and it didn't take long. In March of 2006, Mike Akatiff and his crew boarded a plane for Lake Gairdner, Australia. My pass of 289 mph coasting through the lights with a blown motor was still the fastest pass on two wheels down under.

Jimmy Odom and Mike Akatiff parted ways over the off-season. John Noonan would be the new pilot and Sam Wheeler was asked to go along as the backup driver. When they arrived, conditions weren't to their liking and their best wasn't good enough to beat my mark. The wind and rain had left the salt in bad shape and a run of 249 mph was the best they could muster. It was a silent victory for me, but the story keeps getting better.

Upon their arrival back in the states, Mike Akatiff sent me an e-mail stating that they were considering other drivers for the upcoming 2006 Bonneville season. They wanted to know if I'd consider driving the *Ack Attack* streamliner!

My dream of holding the world land speed record was still alive.

I met with Mike and his crew at their San Jose headquarters. My brother and my new wife came along. The decision of driving with a new team on a bike I was unfamiliar with wasn't cut and dried. First off, Mike hadn't actually given me the job, but said it was a consideration he would have to take up with his crew. Luckily, Ken Puccio was the crew chief and remembered me from my Speedway racing days. His son even came to one of my racing schools many years back. It was good to have him on my side.

My brother and I went over the bike from head to toe, asking questions about things we didn't understand and filling Mike in on our backgrounds. I'm not considered tall by any means, but compared to the former drivers I guess I was the tallest to be strapped in. If I were to get the job, changes would have to be made. First off, I couldn't use the brakes or the gear shift lever without modifications being made to allow my longer legs to fit within the tight confines of the tubular chassis. The seat would also have to be altered to allow me to sit farther back. This might or might not have an effect on my ability to reach the steering controls properly. Time would tell . . .

My wife was also asked about her thoughts of me driving such a fast and potentially dangerous machine. She has always stood by my side and would back me up if this was something I chose to do. She knew how much having the record meant to me, and also how disappointed I was with losing my ride when BUB unexpectedly let me go. "As long as we have full medical coverage, if that's what he wants to do, that's okay with me."

There. She said it. I officially had her permission.

I met with the Ryans, owners of Top-1 Oil Products, the team's corporate sponsor. They were a fun group and we seemed to hit it off well enough. I hoped to one day have their logo emblazoned across my chest and be racing into the record books in the *Ack Attack* streamliner. It's funny how things can change so quickly. I was alive again. I had my dream back . . .

Before we left, Mike told me that he was arranging a meeting with the crew. If they were on board with having me as their driver, that would be the determining factor. He would go along with their decision either way.

Luckily, a few days later I got my answer. They were the longest few days of my life! As it turned out, everyone was on board with the idea. I would be the new driver.

The next step was to meet at Top-1 Oil's headquarters in the bay area. All the legalities had to be put onto the table and what level of commitment we could expect from our sponsor. They made us feel very welcome right away. Their office was several stories up and the exterior walls were solid glass. These guys were big time.

Fortunately for me, Tricia demanded we have adequate medical coverage if we were to go racing. I hadn't made a big deal about it, but it was the determining factor for her. Leave it to a woman to start making sense when all you want to do is go racing. I have to say, she was in the right. At the speeds associated with our sport, anything can happen. It would have been foolish on my part to accept anything less—kudos to my wife for putting her foot down.

We returned to the *Ack Attack* racing headquarters a short time later for the final fitting and to run the bike a few times on the dyno. It was a pleasant surprise how organized the team was and how serious they were about getting it done right.

Ken Puccio jumped in the cockpit of the bike and fired the twin-engine turbocharged goliath motors. The machine was strapped to the dyno but looked like it wanted to bust free every time he revved the motors. After a few clutch adjustments it was my turn inside. The plan was to make a few motor passes on the dyno, shifting through all six gears. It took me a few tries to get the hang of the heavy-pull clutch and to learn how much throttle was needed to keep the machine from stalling on takeoff.

Once I got the hang of it, it was hard to wipe the grin off my face. I mean, this thing has so much power it is unbelievable. I rapped the throttle a couple of times and the thing literally sent chills down my spine. Tricia stood on the sidelines as we simulated a couple of runs, the rear tire spinning furiously against the dyno's metal drum drive roller.

Unlike *Big Red*, this thing fired every time and ran like a champ. It was a less complicated design, but one that worked flawlessly. I was beginning to see the big picture. All this team needs is the right conditions and a capable driver, and the record is theirs. The bike already set an unofficial record of 328 mph at Bonneville in October of 2004. This was done with the engine configuration putting out approximately 600 horsepower. In its current form, the bike is now capable of producing 900 horsepower!

Mike put together a test session to familiarize me with the machine. We would pack our gear and head to Silver Springs to test on the runway of the local airport. The goal was to get a little "seat time" and make a few low-speed passes in the neighborhood of 160 mph.

We arrived at Mike's beachfront house on Lake Tahoe the night before the test and were met by the entire crew. After the nickel tour of Mike's 7,000-square-foot vacation pad, it was off to the garage, where the *Ack Attack* was sitting waiting to be brought to life. The bike was sporting new paint and looked fast just sitting there on the trailer in his garage.

After hooking up the laptop to retrieve data while the engine was running, Mike ordered the crew to fire the bike. The surrounding houses and tall pines echoed with the high-pitched rumble of the double-engined steed. A couple out for an afternoon stroll stopped in their tracks and peered into the garage, unsure of what it was they were seeing. It's not everyday that a 350-mph streamlined motorcycle shows up in your neighborhood and howls angrily with every blip of the throttle.

The laptop showed that the rear engine was starting to run a little hot. The crew removed the carbon fiber bodywork and bled the cooling system. The rear engine didn't react to the changes so they did it a second, and then third time. Mike removed the thermostat and took it inside and put it in boiling water. It was working fine. By almost 1 a.m. the crew had the problem fixed. It was time for bed. Morning reveille was at 3:45 a.m.

Ouch . . .

Morning came way too fast. I stumbled out of bed and crept around the pitch black castle searching for light switches. One by one the crew came to life and walked in zombie mode to the bathroom, where they would make the transformation back to the living. It wasn't long before we found ourselves heading into the Nevada desert in search of the infamous Silver Springs Airport.

Mike stayed behind, along with a magazine reporter that he flew up from the bay area. Together they would jump in his Cessna and meet us there a little later. By plane, the journey was only about 20 minutes—the drive took us an hour and a half. Needless to say, they beat us there.

One thing about the new team, they have style. Mike had the guys bring his Segway scooter for a pit bike. During one of the breaks in the action I got a chance to ride the thing. What a kick! A Segway is a futuristic stand-up, two-wheeled scooter with a gyroscope to keep it from tipping. Nobody told me how to dismount, and when I tried to get off, the damned thing tried to run me over. I think I'm better off sticking to going fast. That *Back to the Future* stuff can hurt you.

After all the anxiety and wondering about the new ride, it was time to find out. The guys strapped me in and positioned me at the far end of the runway pointing straight down the middle. Mike purposely raised the skids a little higher than normal, which made the bike lean over farther than usual. Taking off from a dead start leaning over the way it was would be difficult at best. His thinking was he wanted me to have to work the bike to get it going straight. I would get a better feel for how it reacted and would be forced to manhandle it more than usual. I think he also wanted to see what I was made of; see if I had what it takes to get the job done.

Well . . . my first start wasn't exactly spot-on. I revved the motor to where I thought it should be and let out the clutch. I made it about 5 feet before both motors stalled and I was left leaning on my left skid hoping nobody noticed I hadn't left the staging area. Those Hyabusa motors like to be revved and revved hard. With the lowered compression ratio for the turbo, the motors didn't produce as much torque as they normally would. I knew what I had to do.

The crew restarted the motors and stepped back a second time. I raced the engines and this time kept the revs up high as I disengaged the clutch. Rather than stalling a second time, the rear wheel lit up as I put the hammer down and burned rubber down the runway. John Force had nuthin' on me. I was amazed right away at just how much power my new ride had. Shifting the double engine machine wasn't as easy as most bikes. There were two clutches to disengage, two transmissions to shift, twice as many things to go wrong.

Big Red was computerized and all I had to do was push a button. On the *Ack Attack*, you had to pull in a clutch lever that was so stiff you'd swear carpal tunnel would set in before the lever reached the bar. You had to reach your toes under the foot-operated shift lever and pull hard until both transmissions were engaged. The system works and has never had an electrical failure, because there is nothing electrical about it. Enough said.

My first run was a blast. I just cruised the length of the runway getting a feel for things. It handled pretty good. I got a little off course when I first took off, but that was only because I spun the rear tire a little too much and the rear end came around a tad. I would do better on the next run.

And the next run.

And the next run.

We made about 15 passes in all. The bike performed well all 15 times. I was stoked. *Big Red* is a technical wonder, but it seemed like something was breaking on every test session. On this thing, when we were done, the only thing left to do was load it up and take it home. Maybe give it a bath.

* * *

At Speed Week you aren't allowed to tow a streamlined motorcycle. Because we would be running such tall gearing, it would be difficult to take off from a standing start. Mike designed a parallelogram-shaped contraption that attached to the front of his truck and plugged into the rear of the bike. The idea was to push me from behind with his truck to bring me up to speed (somewhere between 30 and 50 mph) so I could pull the tall gearing and maintain some form of control while dumping the clutch and releasing 900 horsepower of pissed-off turbocharged heat.

To his credit it only took two tries to convince us the contraption worked. My first thought was that if I got a little askew, Mike might run me into the ground and use me for traction. As it turned out, I was able to balance the bike and keep it centered in front of him while he brought me up to speed. He would then radio me to engage the tranny and pull away, which seemed to work effortlessly. Like John Jans from the BUB crew, Mike scored a big "attaboy" for his invention, which worked perfectly from the get-go.

All we needed now was a few miles of salt and a timing light.

The crew and I bonded over pizza and beverages at a nearby parlor after the testing was over. Everyone came away happy. We had a bike that ran well and a crew that kept it in race-ready trim. My job seemed secured by the end of the day, which was a huge load off my mind. Everyone said they thought I handled the bike well and that our chances were good as far as the record was concerned. I asked Mike how he thought the test went. "You're the man," was his official reply.

The ride back home seemed to fly by. All I could think of is what it would feel like being strapped in on the famed Bonneville Salt Flats just a little over a week away—900 horsepower and a bike with virtually no speed limit. Just the thought brought a smile to my face. I only hoped I could pilot the thing as well as my predecessors. Jimmy Odom is no slouch. He made the team proud.

It was my turn now.

Chapter Eighteen
Speed Week 2006

I received an unexpected piece of news while exiting Highway 80 into Wendover. We had just completed the 500-mile journey from Grass Valley to Bonneville. Mike told me that he and the crew were just finishing up replacing the rear motor. I was surprised because it seemed to work so well during our initial test session at the Nevada airstrip. Apparently on our last run the rear motor was somehow engaged in a different gear than the front motor. It over-revved and came apart. The good news was the new engine was fresh and actually shifted better than the one we broke. The crew worked their tails off and got the job done with plenty of time to spare. Pretty neat.

Just a small portion of our gang anticipating the next run. *Photo courtesy of Ed Chamberlain*

August 15, Tuesday morning: I was required to do a licensing run before being allowed to run at full speed, due to only running on private time with my previous team. I'd run once before at Speed Week, but that was several years ago; too long, as far as they were concerned.

To obtain my license I had to maintain a speed of 175–200 through one of the measured miles. Mike did his calculations: At 9,500 rpm in high gear I would run somewhere around 188 mph. I averaged 185 through the first mile . . . good enough.

Going fast (relatively) was the easy part . . . taking off from a worn out starting grid that was slippery and rutted from 500–600 high-powered salt racers was another story. As soon as I released from the push vehicle I began to slip and lean uncontrollably. On a few occasions I thought the *Ack Attack* was going down. Then, as soon as I reached good salt, everything was fine. As I eased on the throttle the bike responded and began pulling like nothing else I ever experienced. I was barely using any power, and reaching 185 mph was really quite easy.

Southern California Timing Association (SCTA) rules say that after you've completed your run you are to turn out to the left and exit the course so the next run can begin. I did so, or so I thought. Actually, I stopped somewhere short of the return road and got an earful from the officials for not exiting the course completely. My excuse was that I'd never had to turn out before and didn't realize just how far off the course the return road was. I thought I was plenty far enough out.

My bad.

I promised it would never happen again—lesson learned. Back in the pits we returned to the registration booth and traded in my rookie card for a license to haul ass. I was a happy camper and couldn't wait for my next run. I felt like a five-year-old who was just given a free pass to the candy store. I was smiling so much my cheeks hurt.

Wednesday. The pits were alive with action. The *Ack Attack* had the rear wheel removed. The low speed tire was replaced with the Mickey Thompson racing slick. Mike asked me what I wanted to do. "Well, 300 is my first goal. I've been close many times but never actually hit the mark,"

Mike typed in some numbers on his laptop. The MoTeC software gave him what he was looking for. "How about if we put a 33-tooth rear sprocket on? At maximum acceleration and peak rpm you would top out somewhere around 362 mph." He scratched his head and waited for my reply. "Of course, that's under perfect conditions . . . "

I looked at him and swallowed hard. "Sure . . . I guess that will work."

"Look, if you only want to go to 300, then only run to fifth gear. At 9,500 rpm you'll be doing about 305 mph." With little thought he continued, "Of course, if everything feels good you could just keep going. 300 . . . 330, there's really not much difference. They're both way too fast."

That would be the tallest gear the bike had run. "What the hell," I thought. "I'm only going to go as fast as I feel comfortable going. It doesn't matter what gear he has on it." The numbers were mind-boggling. Just tossing around the idea of a 330-mph run got me all giddy.

It took several hours to make all the changes and ready the bike to go fast. They put it in line, ready to do business. All that was left to do now was wait.

And wait.

And wait.

Four hours later we were near the front of the line. As fate would have it, just as it was getting near our turn, the wind picked up. We will only run in 5-mph winds or less. Less is better. The wind picked up to 12–15 mph. It got so bad they postponed the meet for the rest of the day. We would get to run early on Thursday.

I was actually pleased with the way it turned out. In the morning the air is cooler and the salt is drier. Things were going our way.

Thursday morning: We got an early start. Everyone was anxious to get to the salt and see what we had. There were about 10 cars from impound that would get to run before they reopened the staging line for our turn. Impound is where you were required to go if your first pass was above the record you were trying to beat. If you had a record pass, your vehicle spent the night in impound and was put at the head of the line the next morning for your return run attempt. I'd never been in impound before and wanted desperately to experience it firsthand.

When it was finally our turn, I felt a little nervous. It was time to put up or shut up. Mike and the crew joked that the driver's name was Velcroed on my race suit and could easily be changed. It was all in fun but I felt like I still had to prove to them that they made the right decision by picking me as the guy to get the job done.

The starter signaled that we were next. He stood about six feet and weighed around 250 pounds. Buzzy and Jim True strapped me in. The starter then came over and checked their handiwork. He gave each belt a stiff tug until my voice was a couple of octaves higher than I cared for. He was just doing his job. Mike positioned the push truck behind me and plugged his two-headed contraption into the rear of the machine. We pulled to the front of the line and picked the smoothest starting position we could find.

This was it.

We were signaled the course was clear. I revved my twin-engined steed a couple of times for good measure as we began rolling down the track. Mike counted off the miles per hour: 20 . . . 30 . . . 40 . . . I pulled in the stiff clutch and popped both engines into gear. I released the clutch and pulled steadily away. I was still a bit uneasy about the rutted starting area, even though they had moved us a mile farther up. I probably could have been a little more aggressive at the beginning, seeing as how the new starting location was considerably better than where I began my licensing run.

Everything went smoothly. I rolled on the throttle and held on tight as the rear tire dug in and spit me forward. At about the 2-mile mark a gust of wind came from the right, blowing me to the left side of the course. I countered and leaned in against it, but lost a little time in the process. As soon as I was past the troublesome area I straightened her out and stretched her legs.

Wow.

The bike seemed to be on rails. The faster I went, the better the bike worked. It was stable at speed and seemed to be working perfectly. The timing lights from the four to the five is the fastest part of the course; the five being where you shut down and hit the chutes. In between the markers I was again hit by a right to left wind that carried me dangerously close to the edge of the course. For a moment it looked like I was going to run into the 5-mile marker. Instead I hit the chutes early and slipped though with very little room to spare. As soon as the three-foot ribboned chute opened I was yanked left, off the course. At first I thought I was in trouble but the *Ack Attack* just soaked up the ungroomed salt without any problems.

The top speed for my first pass was 309 mph.

THREE HUNDRED AND NINE MILES PER HOUR!

Three hundred was a milestone for me and I finally achieved it. When Buzzy and crew showed up and told me my time, we were ecstatic. For nearly eight years with the BUB team, we could only get close. On my first pass with Ack and company we had success. It was amazing how easy it was with such a powerful machine. There is no substitute for raw horsepower. The *Ack Attack* has more than any other two-wheeled, piston-driven streamliner competing today.

I remember as I barreled down the salt, Mike saying it wasn't fast enough. It was like he was right there beside me; with my earphones I could hear him clear as day. At the time I had my hands full just driving the thing and sort of tuned him out. On my ride back to the pits we discussed the run; 309 was good, but we needed to go faster if we wanted the record. Mike was candid about what needed to be done. "You have to go faster sooner. The more speed you gain early on, the faster you will be at the end."

It's really odd having just completed the fastest run of your life—the first time over 300 mph—a lifetime achievement . . . and being told you're still going too slow.

Whoa.

But he was right. We downloaded the data onto the MoTeC, inspected the bike, and performed routine maintenance before putting her back in line. I knew what I had to do and felt confident I could improve on my next pass.

At around three o'clock we shoved off for our second run. I was able to accelerate a little better than last time but struggled even more with the wind. As it turned out, we had a 6-mph wind coming from the east that was really cramping my style. The more I tried to lean into it, the more it pushed me from right to left. When I was finally past the troublesome area I screwed her on and tried to make up time. By the time I reached the far end of the course the wind returned and I found myself once again off the side of the course after deploying the parachute. This time I was able to at least accelerate all the way through the trap, increasing my speed to a 314-mph average through the measured mile with a 321.875 exit speed. I was now within fractions of the current world land speed record—and it only took two passes to do it.

Friday morning: The plan was to drag race all the way to the 2-mile marker. This way, if we carried our momentum, by the end of the run we should be able to put a big number on the board. We would hit it hard right from the start and hope to God that we could keep it between the lines. Sounded easy enough . . .

From the start I knew what I had to do. As soon as I pulled away from the push vehicle, I found myself pushing harder than ever before. A couple of times the rear tire broke loose and spun so hard I was concerned I might over-rev the motors and bring my run to a premature end. That same nasty side wind hit me but I recovered early and set my sights on the measured mile. The course was rutted and bumpy from the 500-plus cars ripping it up. I stayed in the throttle all the way, spinning and drifting, but for the most part just hauling ass. Man did it feel good. At the 5-mile shut-off, the wind was gone, and it seemed easy to keep the bike centered through the lights and out the exit. When I pulled the chutes they hit hard, harder than I've ever felt on this machine. I knew then that we were going pretty fast.

I pulled left and ran through the ungroomed salt in search of the return road. Like the Energizer Bunny, I kept going and going, but couldn't find my mark. We had gone so fast that we literally used up the entire course and then some getting her stopped. There were no more markers—or even a return road that far down the salt.

Hmmm.

Mary True and a few others came running toward me out of nowhere. They had their arms raised and were screaming with excitement. More crewmembers joined in, all with big grins across their faces. Mary asked me if I knew how fast I'd gone. I knew it was pretty good, but without a speedometer to verify, I wasn't really sure. "You went a 329 average through the lights with a 338 exit speed," Mary proudly announced.

Little did I know at the time that I had just made the fastest run ever recorded on two wheels . . . and it only took three passes to get there. I thanked God for bringing me home safely, Mike for giving me the opportunity, and anyone else who would listen. I was one happy camper.

On the drive back to the pits—or should I say, on the drive to impound (yee-haw)—Mike asked me if at any time I was ever out of control. His big duallie push truck was full of crewmembers. I looked at him from the rear seat and said: "Only when I said 'yes' to driving for you." Everyone busted up. I was so happy. The reigning champion and fastest ever on two wheels.

Somebody pinch me . . .

While the crew readied the bike for our return run, I was dropped off at our pits so I could rest in the shade and cool off a bit. I called my dad and told him what we had just done. I was getting choked up just talking about it. He was so proud he told me the tears were running down his face. I called my brother next. We talked about the run in detail; he likes the details. I told him we had another run to make, to try and break the current SCTA/BNI record. Sure, I wanted to break their current record, which was actually faster than the real Fédération Internationale de Motocyclisme (FIM) world record, but my ultimate goal all along was the title of World Record Holder. That would have to wait until two weeks later at the BUB event. The FIM would be there. Everything else was just filler. That's where we needed to shine.

Mike and I discussed strategies. My speeds early on were much better than before. At the end of the run the bike was still pulling strong and still accelerating hard. Most machines reach a plateau and sort of run out of steam by the end. Not the *Ack Attack*. If we had another mile I'm sure the bike would have gained another 20 or 30 miles per hour . . . maybe even more. I sat in the shade surrounded by my wife, my daughter, my mom, and my friends. There was no place I'd rather be.

Tricia was on the cell phone talking to her dad. Her voice was animated and full of zing. She was so proud of what we'd done. Her voice was shaking but she filled him in on every detail. He loved hearing his daughter so excited. He was happy for me; even more so for her. Next thing you know she's stuffing her cell phone in my hand, "Here, my dad wants to talk to you."

She looked so happy and proud. I put the phone to my ear waiting to be congratulated. "So," he said calmly as if just waking from a peaceful nap, "what's new with you?" I about fell out of my chair. Leave it to my father-in-law to be the town clown.

Moments later Mike showed up with the duallie and told me it was time. I grabbed my gear and squeezed in among the rest of the crew. We motored down to impound and followed the official to the starting line. We were the fastest in a small group of diehard racers that made it all the way to the final day of the meet and through impound for a final shot at history. Since this was the last day of the meet, if you made a run above the existing record, you went straight to impound until the rest of the runs were over. Under the watchful eye of the SCTA, we caravanned to the starting line. No waiting until the next day. Again, it looked like things were going our way.

But it was not meant to be.

On my final run, it started off perfectly. I ran fast right away, spinning and slipping but putting down some serious numbers. Right off we were faster than even my best run. But somewhere between the 2- and 3-mile mark the bike started making a strange sound. The top end also felt a little blubbery. For the first time, I felt a slight vibration on a machine that up until now felt like it was running on electric power. Something wasn't right. I knew we were going well, and I could probably walk away with the SCTA/BNI record if I just ignored it and kept the hammer down.

Instead I chose to abort.

As much as I wanted to continue, my goal and the team's ultimate goal is the world record. If I destroyed the bike on this run we might miss our shot at the record only two weeks away. At about the 3-mile mark I radioed that I was aborting the run and threw out the laundry. I was already traveling at over 300 mph. What a shame, we were so close.

When the crew caught up to me they asked what happened. I explained the peculiar sound and how the motors didn't seem right on top end. They popped off the upper shell so they could get a visual on what was going on. At first everything appeared to be fine.

"Let's fire up the motors individuallie," Jim Leal, a crewmember, said. Someone hit the starter on motor one. Everything seemed perfect. They killed the engine and lit number two . . . there it was. The exhaust wrap was blown off around the header and was leaking badly. It also had a different sound and a different idle speed than before. "Either the exhaust came loose or the header broke," Mike said. "You did the right thing, Rocky."

I had my doubts. If I had just kept going, who knows? I was pleased that they found something and that it wasn't just me. The original plan was to leave the bike in an airplane hangar in Wendover until the BUB meet. Now there was work to do. The bike would be taken back home and a new exhaust system manufactured—the entire bike would be gone through from head to toe, all for the best. We would be more than ready for the BUB meet. Like I said before, things seemed to be going our way.

When we left the salt that afternoon we had made the fastest run on two wheels in recorded history. We were in the driver's seat going into the next meet, where it all counted. The drive home was filled with happy thoughts and memories. The next two weeks would be the longest ever, but anything worth having is worth waiting for . . .

Chapter Nineteen
Feeling the Heat

Like most competitions, there is a heated rivalry going on inside and outside the arena. As much as I wish it were a friendly one, there was no such luck here. After being blown off course twice out of four runs at over 300 mph at Speed Week, it got me thinking about the upcoming event: The International Motorcycle Speed Trials, which is being promoted by my former employer and team owner, Denis Manning.

Every tenth of a mile, on either side of his course, in his event, he uses banners made from a PVC pipe frame with a colored flag draped over the framework, which is pounded into two holes

The *Top-1 Ack Attack* sits waiting for action. *Photo courtesy Tricia Robinson* drilled in the salt. If the course is 10 miles in length, that would be approximately 200 flags pounded in the salt on either side. That's 200 chances to hit something if the run was to go wrong.

All of the bigger meets use a black line on either side of the course and only use the framed banners at each measured mile. It is much safer with much less to hit out there. Motorcycle streamliners are affected much more by crosswinds than traditional bikes because of the greater side area of their composite bodies.

Landracing.com is a popular website for salt racers to discuss topics regarding upcoming events, safety issues, and the need for speed. There is a message board specifically dedicated to the BUB International Motorcycle Speed Trials event. I posted my concerns having just returned from Speed Week and having personally been blown off course at high speeds. It was basically a discussion about the benefit of using the black lines over the plastic framed flags. Other forum members offered their opinions and, for the most part, agreed with me. Ultimately, safety was the issue at hand.

A few days later I heard from my team owner and from several other acquaintances that my post infuriated Mr. Manning. Though that was in no way my intention, at least it got his attention. I hoped maybe he would see the light and try and improve the safety of his event for the sake of all those who supported him and chose to compete at his event.

Instead, his remarks suggested that the plastic-framed course markers would be used just to make me nervous, and that somehow I insulted him by my comments. He made it clear to everyone who would listen that he was infuriated with me. In technical terms, I was on his shitlist. At this point, we hadn't spoken since parting ways, but I had hoped that we could at least be civil when it came to our common interest of bringing home the record. As it stood, the gloves were coming off and it would be an all-out brawl to the end.

I had the utmost respect for the members of his team and all the hard work they've done. I had been one of them until recently. But, in regards to Manning and his unwillingness to embrace ideas other than his own, especially in the name of safety, I stood firm in my beliefs. If it was a war that he wanted, it was a war he'd get.

May the best team win.

Chapter Twenty
International Motorcycle Speed Trials: Making History

Have you ever had one of those days when things just seemed to go your way? September 3, 2006, was it for me. It didn't start out that way—in fact, it started out rather crummy. I spent the previous night tossing and turning unable to sleep. Our room was adjacent to the registration desk, not far from the main entrance. People were coming and going throughout the night. I know because I heard every one of them.

The completion of our second run. We had just broken the world land speed record. Most of the crew hadn't made it back from the other end of the course yet to celebrate. *Photo courtesy of Meggan Bechtol*

When I got out of bed, my head was in a fog and I was possibly a shade on the irritable side. But things got better quickly. After feasting on coffee, half a stale bagel, and greasy sausage, I at least knew my system was regular.

We had rented a mini van for the journey so we could drive directly onto the salt. Buzzy, his wife Jill, Tricia, and I motored toward the rising sun with Eminem's "Lose Yourself" blaring on the CD. I'm not particularly fond of rap, however the words to this particular song were inspirational to me and the gang. We played it every chance we got.

"Look . . . if you had one shot . . . one opportunity . . . to seize everything you ever wanted . . . one moment . . . would you capture it? Or just let it slip?"

Man, that's me he's talking to. His life . . . my life. Sometimes you only get one shot. This was mine. Great stuff. He made me want it even more. Thanks, Eminem.

The sunrise was spectacular. We cruised the salt bed at 75 mph, the mini van humming as a fine spray of dry salt plumed behind. The flags marking the course blew gently in the morning breeze. Yes, I said flags. Red course markers . . . lots of them. Manning won. He was going to do things his way in spite of the obvious safety concerns. I smiled as we picked up speed running alongside the 11-mile course. I noticed there was also a crooked black line on either side. In some areas there were dashes, in others no lines at all. I don't know what the hell he was thinking. That's my whole point . . . he probably wasn't.

Our pit area was easy to find. Nine blue pop-up tents with yellow and red "Top-1" logos emblazoned across the top stood out remarkably well. Beside that was a canvas-covered structure with our open trailer parked beneath, keeping the bike hidden from the sun's harsh rays. To the left was an oversized motor home that was used to prepare all the meals for the crew while on the salt. A box trailer was on the other side housing additional equipment. There were also vans, rental cars, motorcycles, and the like. We had the largest and nicest pit area of the entire meet.

And of course, we had the misters running to keep us cool.

Buzzy, my right hand man, had been recently stung between the eyes by a bee, and his face was so swollen that his eyes were little more than puffy slits. This was the guy who would be packing the parachutes before each run and strapping me in along with Jim True. This happened the day before we were scheduled to head for Bonneville and luckily it was steadily getting better. Staying home was never an option. I put my life in his hands when I'm out there and I trust him completely. I wouldn't do it without him.

When we arrived at the pits, Mike and the crew were making a few final adjustments to the bike. Apparently they had changed the gearing since this course was a little longer than the 7-mile course we ran at Speed Week a couple of weeks earlier.

Technically, it was only 1 mile longer as far as bike preparation was concerned. At Speed Week, even though the course was 7 miles long, the measured mile where the timing lights were tripped was from the 4 to the 6 with a 2-mile shut-off. For this meet, the 11-mile course was divided evenly. The measured mile was from the 5 to the 6, giving us 1 extra mile to accelerate before a 5-mile shut-off. This was because Fédération Internationale de Motocyclisme (FIM) rules require you to run one pass in each direction and the average speed of the two runs needs to be one percent over the existing record. At Speed Week, you still had to post an average of two runs, but the course was run in only one direction heading away from Highway 80 for safety reasons.

At this particular meet, having a full 11 miles to run on—which doesn't happen very often—there was plenty of room to get her stopped in either direction. The conditions of the track seemed excellent. Pete Davis, a good friend and former coworker, groomed the course and provided a world class testing ground for us to compete on. My hat's off to him for doing such an excellent job.

Back to the gearing.

I asked Mike just how much gear he put on. He smiled at me and said not to worry about it. "Just go out there and go fast, Rocky," he said with a confident smile. "If it feels good just go for it. If it doesn't . . . you're the one in control. It's up to you."

At times I thought Mike would make a good politician. He could talk to me and I could see his lips moving, but he didn't really say anything. But the smile . . . that said it all. Whatever it was, it was geared to go plenty fast.

I looked around for Dave Dahlgren, our MoTeC guru. Sure enough he had his laptop connected to the bike and was going over the data. I stood next to him for nearly 10 minutes while he studied the graphs and charts and did his best to make sense of it all. "How fast are we geared for?" I asked.

Dave looked up from the screen. "I don't know. Mike has those figures. You should ask him." Dave's expression gave very little away. He'd make a hell of a poker player. This guy seems to know everything. He turned back to his laptop and continued with his business. Hmmm.

At this particular meet a rare opportunity presented itself. For the first time, four streamliners would be battling head to head for the ultimate reward: bragging rights as the world's fastest. Max Lambky and crew would be competing with their twin-engine Vincent streamliner, while my former ride, the BUB team, would be running *Big Red* with Chris Carr at the controls. Sam Wheeler, the current world's fastest with a 332.410-mph two-way pass, would be running for top honors as well. The *Ack Attack* was up for the challenge. Dave Campos, the FIM record holder at 322.149, could do little more than stand by and watch as history was about to be changed.

Our plan was to come out swinging. We wanted to run early and take advantage of the good conditions. You never knew when the wind might pick up or the lingering clouds hovering over the surrounding mountains might decide to rain on your parade. Sunday, September 3, was the official start of the meet. After the riders' meeting, the track was officially opened for business at noon.

We paraded to the starting line followed closely by an international procession of media personnel that was unlike any I'd seen before in the sport of land speed racing. The routine of off-loading the bike from the trailer and shoving five bags of ice into the intercooler became a never-ending ritual: the colder the better. If we had to wait any time at all, the water would be drained and more ice added. Anything in the name of horsepower.

I suited up while tiptoeing between cameramen and reporters. I swear they must have got 10 different shots of me tying my shoes. The conditions were to our liking so I jumped in the bike while Buzzy and Jim yanked on the straps until I could hardly move. We were one of the first to run on the long track; definitely the first streamliner. Mike plugged the two-headed contraption into the back of the bike and requested a final wind check before pushing me off.

The first course marker was at the quarter-mile mark. This was significant in that whether you were being towed or pushed, you had to release and be under your own power before reaching this mark. If you were still connected past the mark it was grounds for disqualification.

Mike accelerated behind me pushing me up to speed while calling out the miles per hour so I would know when to disengage. At 45 mph, I revved the engine hard and pulled back on the shift lever until both engines were engaged. You could tell the gearing was much taller by how the bike reacted. It had enough power to pull the gear but was at the bottom of the power curve when I initially released.

"The gear is up," Mike yelled into the center of my brain. My ear jacks go way inside my ear and I can hear every breath, every curse, every comment he makes like he's inside my head. Even though I have a green light on the dash, it's nice to know those things aren't still out there only inches above the salt while I'm picking up speed.

It doesn't take long for the *Ack Attack* to come to life. The bigger gear seems to take longer to rev out, but when it does and the shift light comes on, you're hauling ass. I try my best to accelerate hard and stay in it, even though the lower gears are tricky due to wheelspin at the slower speeds. I press firmly against the shifter and engage second gear cleanly. I roll back into it and watch the tach climb as the motors hum like a finely tuned instrument. My eyes are wide with excitement as the rear tire breaks loose and the back end starts to come around. The rpm race as the tire spins frantically on top of the loose salt.

I roll out of it slightly and then right back in. Holy shit . . . that was close. Moments later the shift light returns and I hit third.

Then fourth.

Fifth is next. By now I'm flying. I battle a slight right to left crosswind, but for most of the run it's coming directly at me. Headwinds aren't bad. No wind is better. By the 4-mile marker it's time to line up and execute. It's a drag race through the lights. I have to be in high gear before reaching the lights so as not to waste time shifting where it counts. By the 4½ I reach the final cog. This thing is screaming.

I had concerns about hitting the chutes at these higher speeds, because they hit so hard the harness literally digs into you. I suppose that's better than flying through the front windshield as the rest of the bike scrubs off speed at an intense pace. I was going to ask Mike earlier what he thought about it, and then realized no one had gone these speeds before. There was no one to ask. I would just have to find out for myself.

Luckily, I was able to run pretty much down the center of the course through the measured mile, so I wasn't too concerned about running off course and into Manning's damned red flags. Usually I hit the chutes with the throttle on and run it out till they hit. The idea is to not let the weight transfer from the rear wheel to the front from all the aerodynamic drag created at such high speeds. Too much weight on the front end could possibly cause the front tire to fail or the suspension to become overloaded. I didn't really want to find out what it might do, but at the same time I wasn't too crazy about taking such a large "hit" and overstressing the bike and myself as the chutes filled with air and I hit the proverbial "wall."

I tried something a little different from my normal routine, which worked out nicely. As I broke the final light at speeds approaching 350 mph, I rolled slowly out of the throttle, being careful not to let it get away from me. I could feel the nose starting to dip, but kept her pointed down the middle of the course. After coasting down for half to three-quarters of a mile, I released the chutes and planted my feet against the front bulkhead and pushed with all my might. I buried myself in the back of the seat pan and held on as the air brake took over.

It worked pretty well, and I was able to slow to a comfortable pace and cruise at a couple hundred miles an hour to the far end of the course. I knew we were at record pace because the run was clean with no major problems. With the extra gear and the longer course, I knew the speeds would be up from my previous runs at Speed Week. Impound was at the very end, just off to the left. I steered the *Top-1 Oil Ack Attack* directly at the Impound Tent and pulled alongside, parking only a couple of feet away. The officials danced around looking a bit nervous before realizing I actually knew what I was doing.

Off the trailer, our average speed through the measured mile was 344.673 mph. It was our first run and was already the fastest run ever recorded in the history of two-wheeled land speed racing. Not bad . . .

The rules say you have two hours from the time you trip the light in the measured mile till your return run, which also must trip the same light within the allotted timeframe. Our crew hustled and had the bike ready in about 30 minutes. They were so fast that by the time I got my race suit off and was standing in my shorts and a T-shirt trying to cool off, they told me to get dressed and get back in the bike. As I mentioned before, the press was everywhere. And yes, they got more opportunities after the interviews to film me tying my shoes once again.

I couldn't believe how things were going. That first run seemed easy enough. Another one like that and we'd be in the record books. I watched as they crammed five more bags of ice into the intercooler and motioned me forward. All of a sudden my nerves started playing games with me. "Don't screw this one up," I told myself. There were only 11 miles of salt and a set of timing lights between me and the new world record.

Sixteen years.

Dave Campos, the fastest man in the world on two wheels, watched from the sidelines. My mom and my wife held their breath as did the rest of our team on pit row. My brother and his wife, who flew from Salinas to watch us make history, had broken down not far away and had to stop for repairs. They wouldn't be there to witness it, should we hit our mark.

I asked Mike for a wind report. It was only 2 to 3 miles an hour at a quartering tailwind. Not bad, I thought. As Buzzy and Jim strapped me in, I noticed how tight they were securing me. Holy crap, was it tight. I guess they knew this was the big one. They knew I would be going for it no matter what. They didn't have to say anything; we all knew what was going on. The air was filled with tension. I could feel my hair turning grayer by the minute.

Buzzy looked at me with this silly smile. "Did I ever tell you the one about Sven, Olley, and Ole?" He has this same old joke he always uses whenever things get a little tense. The thing of it is, he changes it every time. It's so stupid that it's funny. I guess that's the point.

They tug on the straps a final time. I wasn't going anywhere. Jim True looked me in the eye. "This one's going to be a lot of fun," he said, kind of like Buzzy with his Olley and Ole routine. He smiled a knowing smile. Jim's been there. He holds a few records himself, only on four wheels instead of two. "Just go out there and enjoy it. Have some fun."

What can I tell you? I work with some of the greatest people on the planet. Mike did a radio check before they buttoned down the canopy and we noticed that something has gone wrong with our communication system. I could barely hear him. Once the engines are lit I knew I'd be on my own. We agreed to go on without communication. I had to make sure I released before the quarter-mile marker, and I made a mental note to check the light on the right side of the dash confirming the skids had fully retracted.

The hatch was lowered and latched into place. The first thing I noticed was that I was staring directly into the sun. Up until now, I'd been shaded by a large Top-1 Oil umbrella and hadn't given it a second thought. We lit the engines and, as expected, I couldn't hear a word Mike was saying. I felt the wheels start to roll and took a deep breath.

I asked the big guy upstairs to bring me home safely. He's always been good to me before. I told myself, "Don't screw this one up . . ."

Sixteen years. Man . . .

Nearing the quarter-mile marker on the other end of the track, I revved the engines and pulled hard on the shift lever. Both neutral lights disappeared and I felt the motor lurch beneath me. I rolled on the throttle as Mike and his black Dodge disappeared in my salty wake. I flipped the skid switch up as I rolled the throttle on steadily. The green light illuminated; it was time to go fast.

"This one's going to be a lot of fun." Boy, he wasn't kidding. The bike ran like a top, singing at the top of its powerful lungs. I never broke loose as hard as I did on the initial run, yet overall I couldn't seem to find as much grip as I did earlier on. For some reason, the return run wasn't quite as fast as the opening run on the other side. The sun was blinding me and it was actually a little difficult finding my way back. Several of the mile markers had folded over from being poorly secured, making it difficult to see them. Between the sun and the markers—and the curving random lines, you had to really focus to stay centered on the track.

It was a difficult run and I only managed about 75 percent throttle through the measured mile. The good news was there was still plenty left. I centered myself on the course and rolled out of the throttle once again. When it came time to deploy the chutes, for some reason they didn't want to come out. What usually takes two to three pulls on the mechanical lever somehow wasn't enough. I tried again. Nothing. We have an emergency switch with an explosive deployment mechanism guaranteed to release all the laundry if needed. I pulled the lever once more for good luck before resorting to drastic measures. This time it worked perfectly. It took five pulls to make it happen. We would be discussing this in the pits later . . .

I decided to run her all the way to the other end, to where our initial run began. At around 80–90 mph, I ran over a rough stretch of salt and the front end began to chatter. I thought it was from the bumpy ground but it continued to chatter long after that. I made a mental note to also bring this up while I had the crew's attention.

With only 1 mile to go I could see people in blue shirts jumping up and down waving their arms. I knew we had a good run but it was only then that I realized we had just made history. Our return run was 340.922 mph, giving us a new world record with an official average speed of 342.797 mph! We had just upped the existing record by more than 20 mph.

As I coasted to a stop, the press surrounded me. My crew, who were still coming in, were embracing each other and high-fiving the living hell out of anything that would move. My wife and son Mario, along with my mom and about 30 of our closest friends, had to beeline it from the pits to the end of the course where we were, some 5 miles away. Mario, who is only 15 and has yet to take driver training, also put in a personal best run, maxing out the mini van at 100 mph en route.

As I loosened my harness and disconnected the air hose that feeds clean air into my helmet, it began to sink in. We did it. I yanked the wires from my helmet that connected me to Mike and the crew. It didn't work anyway. The canopy was removed and I was pulled from the tight confines of the metal cockpit and allowed to sit atop the bike with my feet still inside only now directly below me. I raised my fists in victory as the cameras flashed and the cheers began.

Mike Akatiff and his hard-working crew had enabled me to break the world land speed record piloting the *Top-1 Ack Attack* streamliner—the world's fastest motorcycle. The history books would have to be rewritten. THE WORLD'S FASTEST. We had broken a record that stood for 16 years. A record everyone was gunning for but no one was able to officially beat. We were the first to do so. That part will never change.

It was exactly as the man said.

"Boy, did we have some fun!"

Chapter Twenty-One
Crushed Ice

I overheard Dave Campos describe what it felt like to hold the world land speed record for motorcycles. "Imagine having your hands tied behind your back while standing on a block of ice with a noose around your neck." It was an interesting analogy.

We broke Dave's record on September 3, 2006, by over 20 mph. I then inherited the proverbial noose and melting block of ice. The new world record was now 342.797 mph. Don Vesco set the record before Dave Campos at 318.598 mph, which stood for 19 years. Dave then took it to 322.150, upping the record by

Buzzy and my wife catch up with me after breaking the record. It was an emotional moment for all of us. *Photo courtesy of Meggan Bechtol*

4 mph. We added another 20 mph on top of that.

No sooner had I assumed the position on top of the world and atop the melting cube of ice, my footing began to slip. We broke the record on a Sunday, only to have it taken away two days later on a Tuesday.

Chris Carr, driving for my former team in a streamliner that I helped develop, made a first pass at just over 354 mph, the fastest speed ever recorded on two wheels. The run wasn't without controversy. From our pit we watched as *Big Red* ran through the measured mile. It didn't appear to be going that fast, and we all listened in disbelief as his time was announced over the BUB Enterprises PA system, which was nonexistent until his run. It appeared as if he shut off and coasted through the final third of the measured mile, scrubbing off precious speed. How he was able to record such a fast time still baffles me to this day.

Having said that, let me be the first to say I have the utmost respect and admiration for Carr. He is a proven champion on and off the racetrack. On his return run, he achieved a 346.937-mph average through the measured mile which was just awesome. He managed to maintain his speed while battling a pretty nasty crosswind. My hat's off to him for doing such a magnificent job.

His handwritten time slip verified he was the new world record holder. All hail the new king. My time on top was short-lived, but at least it was our team, the *Top-1 Ack Attack* team that was first to break the long-standing record.

* * *

We weren't about to give up without a fight. Mike rallied the troops and we lined up at the starting grid once again. The *Ack Attack* had yet to run at its full potential. There would be no more holding back.

From the start I knew what we had to do. I was determined to run her at full throttle; not an easy task with a bike capable of

900 horsepower—most of it being produced somewhere between 8,000 and 10,000 rpm.

We did exactly that. My run through the lights produced a 347.326 average, our fastest run yet. "Mike, I gave her everything she had," I confessed. "I think she started lying down a little toward the end." Mike massaged his chin while the gears turned inside his head. It was almost like watching a cartoon where the light bulb suddenly appears over the smart guy's head when he's got a brilliant idea. He disappeared into the cab of his truck and buried himself in graphs and charts brought up on the screen of his laptop.

The wizard worked his magic, and then reemerged looking refreshed and hopeful. "I think I know the problem." He placed the laptop on the hood of his truck and dialed his cell phone. Dave Dahlgren, the MoTeC guru, was on the other end. They bantered back and forth while Mike tapped away at the keypad.

"What's going on?" I interrupted.

"I think Dave accidentally went the wrong way when he was leaning out the fuel mixture on the MoTeC, he said. "He was supposed to take out three percent, which would have meant he would have had to enter a 'negative three.' The bike was already running rich. He actually *added* three percent to the fuel mixture. Look, there is no minus sign in front of the three."

The days of jet wrenches and plug readings were long gone. Mike readjusted the fuel settings with the stroke of a few keys. "You really think that's the problem?"

Mike gave a knowing smile. "Sure. That thing was running dead rich. We were giving away a bunch of horsepower. I leaned it back out the three percent and then went a little more. You'll notice a definite difference." Dave had to leave Bonneville on business, but was only a phone call away. Together he and Mike were certain this would be an improvement.

A little over 5 miles away, Carr waited with his crew. Their plan was not to run unless they had to. Their rear tire had chunked pretty badly. A new one would have to be installed and balanced before they could even think about returning to the salt. Chris adjusted his footing on the melting block of ice.

Our return run was the fastest yet, the *Top-1 Ack Attack* posting a 349.031 mph average through the lights heading toward highway 80 with Floating Mountain disappearing in the distance. The course was consistently slower running in this direction. Carr's return run was only 346.937.

We were back. The minor fuel adjustments Mike had made seemed to be working. He would fine-tune his adjustments while the crew readied the bike for yet another run. Our plan was to drop our previous 347 run, leaving the 349 pass as our first run. The rules stated that any two consecutive runs completed within the two-hour timeframe would be allowed as an official record attempt. We had two hours to back it up and hopefully restore our place in history.

The BUB crew could do nothing more than wait and hope.

As fate would have it, an afternoon wind picked up that refused to die. We considered trying our luck a couple of times, but it was just too risky. An annoying headwind with quartering gusts from 5 to 10 miles an hour moved in and set up camp. We watched anxiously as the first hour came and went. Several times we thought about suiting up and taking our chances, but cooler heads prevailed. Jimmy Odom was lucky to walk away from a high-speed crash he had no business running in. It wouldn't happen again.

As much as we hated to do so, we packed our things and returned to the pits unable to defend our title. Our time had run out. The BUB crew breathed a sigh of relief.

Mike and the crew decided to tear into the bike and see how things were holding up. I was of little use to them so I caught a ride back to the hotel to collect my thoughts. It had been one hell of a day. When we arrived that morning we were still the fastest two-wheeled racing team ever to set foot on the salt. We were living the dream. By the end of the day we were second best. It was hard to swallow. I didn't think it would get to me the way it did, but the honest truth of the matter was I was crushed.

My wife and I walked silently to our room. I don't think she knew what to say to me. She knew how hard we worked to get to where we were. How I was more than willing to hurl myself down the salt at ungodly speeds risking life and limb just to say we did it better than anybody else. How appreciative I was to just have this opportunity. How afraid I was to ever let it pass me by. She kept to herself.

We were both exhausted.

I plopped on the bed next to the window. My mind raced with negativity. I hated what had happened . . . hated myself. I was embarrassed to be seen by anybody. I remember how long the walk seemed through the casino and up to our room. The last time I made that journey I had spring in my step and a smile on my face. I wasn't smiling now.

Somewhere in my misery I dosed off. When I awoke I decided to put things in perspective. Here I was feeling sorry for myself and the meet wasn't even over yet. I decided I would turn all my thoughts into positive energy. Whether we walked away with the record or not, it would not be for lack of trying. From that moment on things got easier. Sure, I was disappointed, but I was no longer angry with myself. I would do whatever I could to make us win. I knew Mike would do the same.

Over dinner we discussed several different scenarios that we hoped would make us run faster. We talked about gearing, and how maybe we were trying to pull too much gear. One tooth lower might allow the bike to rev more and pull stronger. We thought we were on to something.

That's when Mike showed up.

He had a pleasant look about him. He knew something we didn't. "I just got off the phone with Dahlgren again. I thought we were running as much boost as we could," his smile widened. "Turns out there's plenty left. We're going to turn her way up tomorrow. I think we can get another 200 horsepower." Now everybody was smiling. "To hell with the gearing," I thought.

The crew went to bed inspired. We were still in the game.

I couldn't believe how upbeat I was the next morning. I mean, the previous night, as ridiculous as it sounds, I had to go through a state of mourning. I had to hit bottom before I could mentally pick myself back up. Breakfast was great. The drive to the salt just fine. Eminem shouted at me through the minivan speakers that this was my shot and to not miss my chance. He was coming through loud and clear.

When we arrived the crew still had the bike apart. The drive shaft connecting the rear motor to the counter sprocket had failed and they were searching frantically for a fix. A new chain was installed and the shaft bearing support reinforced with JB weld. What the hell . . . it was too late to turn back now. At the far end of our pit, a BUB crew member was being helped by one of our guys with their new rear tire. Mike brought a precision balancer that was put to good use helping the competition. I can't say enough about Mike Akatiff. He's the real deal.

On my first start, the bike would hardly run on takeoff and I found myself aborting the run somewhere around the 2-mile mark. Mike had leaned the fuel mixture too much, and the motors refused to run properly on the bottom end.

From the sidelines, we watched as Sam Wheeler barreled down the salt. The Kawasaki-powered *E-Z-Hook* streamliner was hooked up and hauling ass. Sam ripped through the lights with an average speed of 355.303 mph!

These sorts of things just don't happen.

Dave Campos watched from the sidelines as not one, but *three* different streamliners took turns posting the biggest numbers ever recorded in Bonneville's history. The world of motorcycling would be changed forever.

Maybe it was the 11 miles of pristine salt. Maybe technology finally caught up with Joe Teresi and his Easyriders twin-engine Harley-Davidson streamliner. The moon and the stars might have played a role. Whatever the case, the history books would have to be rewritten several times over the course of the Third Annual International Motorcycle Speed Trials.

Sam ran into trouble at the end of his run, his front tire failing at about the same time his parachute deployed at a very high rate of speed. Luckily, he escaped uninjured, though the Kawasaki-powered *E-Z-Hook* streamliner slid on its side for what seemed like an eternity. Mr. Wheeler left with top time of the meet, even though he was unable to back up his run due to his unfortunate incident.

After Mike readjusted the fuel mixture for a final time, we returned to the front of the line as Carr and the BUB crew waited patiently. This time the bike ran great—better than it had all week. The added boost had the motors singing. It felt like we were back on track and I felt confident that we could put down our fastest run yet.

At about the 3-mile, a nasty gust of wind blowing off the levee break hit me unexpectedly. I was pushed off line and headed straight for one of Manning's damned plastic-framed course markers. I tried everything but it was too late. I was either going to take out the marker trying to stay on course, or abort the run and dive outside of it onto ungroomed salt. I chose the latter and found myself fishtailing in the wet, slippery muck. I threw out both chutes and brought her to a quick stop. Damn . . . I thought that would be the one.

It was now the final day of the meet. Thursday, September 7, 2006. At noon the meet would officially come to a close. The only exception would be if anyone were to make their first of two record runs before noon, the mandatory two-hour turnaround timeframe would then come into play.

Like every day before this one, we refused to give up. Mike turned up the boost as high as it would go, 32 pounds, 225 more horsepower then we had on our record run. There was no reason to hold anything back. It was doubtful that our damaged drivetrain could handle the added power, but we decided to throw the dice. If it did, the record would be ours once and for all. I was convinced BUB didn't have anything left to throw at us, or he would have allowed Chris to run earlier.

Talk about stress. I could feel my hair turning gray and the wrinkles tugging at my skin. "Did I ever tell you the one about Sven, Ollie, and Ole?" Buzzy had a grin from ear to ear. I love that guy.

They strapped me in while the BUB crew, which was now stationed down at the starting line next to us, watched in disbelief as we did our best to impersonate the Energizer Bunny. We just kept going and going and . . . If we put up a big number on our down run, they would be forced to run.

Chris suited up and waited.

We fired the bike and prepared to either go down in history or in a ball of flames. I knew there was a better than average chance things could go terribly wrong, but there was also an outside chance we could win. We pushed off and set sail.

The motors ran great, almost too good. By the 3-mile it felt like the bike just went into neutral. My first thought was that the drive shaft finally let go. I coasted to the side of the course and dropped the skids a final time. For us the meet was finally over.

I could picture in my mind the BUB crew popping champagne and beginning their celebration. Who could blame them?

We wheeled our wounded beast back to the pits. Tricia put her arms around me and gave me a big hug. It was difficult to maintain my composure. We'd been through so much. It took a couple of minutes, but I managed to suck it up and accept the fact that we got beat. I was honestly proud of our efforts. The crew kicked ass. I drove at a world-class level. Mike got more out of his equipment and his crew than any other team owner I've ever worked with. We could hold our heads up high, knowing we did our jobs and actually broke the world land speed record which stood for 16 years.

Mike raised his head from the side of the bike. "Hey Rocky, the shaft didn't break. The nut backed off and it just came loose. It was the chain that broke."

It was a good thing I had reached for a Diet Pepsi instead of a beer.

"Let's put on another chain and get back out there. It's not over yet . . . "

Richard Farmer and Howard Carte from the BUB crew ventured over to our pit to congratulate us on such a valiant effort. The last I saw of Howard after he caught wind as to what was going on, he was beating feet back to the BUB pit. There was just over an hour till the official close of the meet. They didn't want to get caught with their pants down should we score a knockout in the final round. The press was going crazy. You couldn't have hired someone to write a better script.

What was interesting was that we made it back to the line with only about 20 minutes to spare. Manning was going nuts. If we made a hot pass, he had to back it up pronto. He must have had a few words with the American Motorcycle Association (AMA) official because he peeked his head into my cockpit just as we were getting ready to run.

"If your pass turns out to be a record run, I need you to exit the course just as fast as you can so Carr will have enough time to defend his run."

"Yeah right," I thought to myself. "What if I got lost or something? Hmmm . . . I wonder what Sven or Ollie or Ole would do . . . "

The BUB pit was alive with action. *Big Red* was lit and warmed up for battle. Denis was shouting orders and looking a little frazzled. Chris was strapped into the machine and told to be ready.

With only 10 minutes left on the clock, we were finally ready to go. We lit off for the final time, a plume of salt spraying behind me as the *Top-1 Ack Attack* gave chase one final time. As bad as we wanted it and as hard as everyone worked to make it happen, by the 4-mile, the drivetrain let go for good. Expensive noises and unfamiliar vibrations filled the cockpit as the wounded streamliner limped through the timing lights with the parachute already trailing behind. This time it really was over.

The BUB crew counted down the seconds until noon, the official cutoff point. They broke out the champagne for a second time, only to be stopped yet again. Charlie Hennekam, the Fédération Internationale de Motocyclisme (FIM) official, informed Denis that because we had broken the clocks before 12 noon, we still had two hours to do a return run and then up until 3 p.m. to try again.

Manning and his crew were floored by the official's statement and couldn't believe what they were hearing. Their reactions were caught on film by the ever-present press, which was actually quite entertaining. Eventually they caught word that we were officially retiring from the event. Who knows if there were any bubbles left in their bottles of champagne?

* * *

Try as we might, our best run of 349.031 wasn't good enough to recapture the record. We had plenty more power available, but a failing driveshaft kept us from utilizing it. Chris Carr left with the record, which we held only days before. Sam Wheeler left knowing he was officially the fastest man on the planet.

The battle is far from over. In fact, it has only just begun. The *Top-1 Ack Attack* team has vowed to return with a vengeance. We will no longer be satisfied to just break the record. No sir . . . been there, done that. We have the 200 MPH Club T Shirt for the 300 Chapter. Still not enough.

Join us on our journey into uncharted territory:

400 mph on two wheels . . . the race of the century!